28

BY SAM WOOD

28

BY SAM WOOD

Change your shape
and change your life
28 minutes for 28 days

with nutritionist Steph Lowe
BSpExSc, GDipHumNutr, NSA

hardie grant books

Contents.

Pleased to meet you

When I was 21 I moved from Tassie to Melbourne to study exercise science, and during my course I was lucky enough to do work experience at a gym. It was there I fell in love with the concept of personal training. I'd always loved staying fit and I love people too, so it came naturally to me. When the week was up, the manager offered me a job. Before I knew it I had 60 appointments a week and was still doing my degree. It wasn't long before I started getting some inquiries from parents who were looking for someone to train their kids. There were two main types I came across: young athletes and kids who were struggling with self-esteem issues. That was where I found a passion I never knew existed. By the time I'd turned 23, I was doing about 100 personal training sessions a week and 30 or so of those were with kids. I was loving every minute of it; I was living and breathing fitness and helping all sorts of people improve their own.

In 2007, I opened Gecko Sports, Australia's first gym specifically for children, and for the next two years that was my life. I concentrated on helping kids with their fitness and growing the business. Then, from that work, I started getting lots of inquiries from mums who needed a personal trainer. I'd come full circle.

My next step was to open the Woodshed, a personal training and small group training studio, where about 30 trainers work closely with our clients. For us it's all about being hands on, and making sure that everyone who steps into that gym is training properly and given the right advice about nutrition so they can achieve the results they need.

It didn't take long for me to realise people are really time poor these days. When you go to the gym, it's not just the time you spend exercising – there's getting there, changing, then getting home again. If you're telling busy people they have to spend an hour exercising, then they add all that extra time on either side, it really starts to add up. The result is people can't or won't commit to as many sessions as is optimum for their health. What I did was develop complete, effective 30-minute sessions – my clients would come in a few times a week, we'd guide them through how to train correctly, then give them some homework (again, a half-hour maximum) to do on the days they weren't here. What it meant was these people were exercising more regularly for less time and seeing some great results.

It works for everyone from young 20-somethings who are just starting out in their careers to 60-year-old CEOs. But the people it especially suits are mums. During my career, I've spent a lot of time with clients and it didn't take me long to realise a lot of women put everyone else's priorities ahead of their own. They take care of the kids, they make sure everything is done for their partners or husbands, and plenty of them also have to keep up with a busy work life. Looking after themselves comes so far down on their list of things to do today that many don't even have the time to think about finding the time to exercise! Give them the opportunity to fit it into their day by making it short and it becomes a lot more manageable.

That's what my team and I did for 15 years – we helped people from all walks of life become the best person they could be by combining exercise with good eating habits.

And then, along came a little television show called *The Bachelor* (where, as many would know, Snezana Markoski became my fiancé). As soon as it finished shooting – and this was even before people were seeing it every week in their homes – I was inundated with inquiries from people wanting to train at the Woodshed. Could they book in? When was I going to open more Woodsheds around the country? The short answer was 'I don't know', and maybe even 'Never'.

But what blew me away was social media and the engagement of these fans online. Maybe I was just behind the curve, but I had never realised what powerful tools the different online programs and apps had become. Be kind; up until that point I'd spent most of my adult life working face to face with my personal training clients.

And that's how *28 by Sam Wood* was born. We've taken our proven program and made it available to everyone, no matter where they live or when they want to exercise.

How does 28 by Sam Wood work?

With the help of my team, I've taken 17 years of experience as a personal trainer and turned it into an online training, nutrition and mindset tool that works. Yes, really. By the time you're reading this book we'll have had more than 100,000 people sign up and do the program.

Each day, we release a 28-minute exercise video that you can do whenever and wherever you can. There are five levels, and you jump in where you think you might fit, then either drop back or go up a level depending on how you go.

Then there's a weekly nutrition plan – it comes out on Thursday, so you can do the shopping on the weekend and get a start on some preparation for the week. Best of all, this is normal, good, tasty food – you can eat it, your partner can eat it, and the kids can eat it – and you shouldn't spend any more than 28 minutes a day cooking either.

The third pillar of the program helps you train your mind the same way you train your body. There are meditations, tips to cope with stress, and visualisations to help you get a good night's sleep every single night. What many people don't realise is that this is as important as finding an exercise program that works for you and changing your daily eating habits to fuel your body properly.

What we hadn't really planned for when we set up 28 was how big a part the community – and there is a very real sense of community among the people who've signed up for the program – would play in people's successes. Mostly, they live in Australia, but there are 28ers all over the world. When people join, they get to become a part of a closed Facebook group where they can ask questions (both of our experts and each other), support one another, organise to meet up on the weekends if they live close by, and share their successes.

So, while I can imagine what it might be like to be a 40-year-old mum with a couple of kids, a part-time job and a million things on her mind, in the Facebook community there are literally hundreds of people who are in exactly *that* situation and have made massive changes to their lives. I can't begin to tell you how powerful that can be. I'd go as far as to say people connect with others in their community in a more powerful way than they might with a personal trainer with whom they work one on one.

Perhaps the most important aspect of *28 by Sam Wood* is that my team and myself – just like you – live in the real world. And we do this program. Remember, this is not about perfection. If you have a beer or a chocolate or miss a workout that's OK. You're human; it happens. What you're working towards is developing a healthy, sustainable way of life.

Work hard and I guarantee you'll see results. In fact, share your triumphs with us and send us an email at hello@28bysamwood.com

Sam

Why my program is different

Chances are you may have tried any number of diets, programs or books available to get your health back on track. Chances are you stuck with them for a while, but eventually went back to old ways. I've talked to many of my clients and they give me plenty of reasons why they couldn't stick with it, but often it boils down to expectations: the expectation that you've got unlimited time and resources to dedicate to losing weight. Unless you're independently wealthy and don't need to work that won't be the case.

For *28 by Sam Wood* we've come up with a program where you cook quick, simple, tasty meals using ingredients you can find at the local shops and dedicate half an hour to exercise every day at whatever time you can fit it in. It's easy and practical. With minimal effort you can make this part of your life. It's authentic and, I promise, it won't drive you insane.

Remember our motto: *progress not perfection*. We live in the real world and recognise you do too.

It's time to move it.

What makes this exercise program so special?

The unique aspect to the workouts I've devised is you can do them anywhere. You don't need to have had any experience working out in a gym because I demonstrate exactly how to perform every single movement, so that you achieve the maximum benefit and avoid injury.

Plus, you're done and dusted in 28 minutes. Simple!

Exercise, and why you'll come to love it

As I mentioned before, I've been a personal trainer for 17 years, and I've worked with thousands of clients of both genders, all ages and from completely different walks of life. But for every 100 clients I meet, 99 of them tell me they have some combination of these goals: lose weight, tone up, feel fitter. The first of those you could achieve by simply changing your eating habits and, for the majority of the time, swapping out your slightly dubious choices for better ones. But you're never going to see a firmer, fitter you unless regular exercise becomes a habit.

And those aren't the only benefits you can look forward to. Are you ready to have more energy, sleep better every night, feel more positive about yourself and cope with the stresses of life better? Regular exercise – and I'm not talking about running marathons or spending hours every day in the gym – can help you achieve all that.

The *28 by Sam Wood* workouts utilise dynamic movements that work the entire body, and improve strength, endurance, mobility and cardiovascular health, making you stronger, leaner and fitter.

Every day we do a different workout, led by me. On Monday, Tuesday, Thursday and Friday they take on a relatively high-intensity, full-body format that has an emphasis on the core. Wednesday is the yin to the rest of the week's yang. We do some gentler, low-impact cardio (the stuff that elevates your heart rate) along with some pilates- and yoga-based movements. These lengthen and stretch the muscles, help with mobility and allow for active recovery in the middle of the training week.

Each of the workouts takes just 28 minutes, plus an important few minutes either side to warm your body up and cool it down again. This helps avoid injuries and some of the normal muscle soreness you feel when you do a good workout.

Based on that same rationale, our weekend workouts are active recovery sessions that you can take outside: walking, jogging, cycling, hiking, running on soft sand, whatever you like really. You can do these workouts on your own, with a friend, other 28ers who live nearby or with your family since, this being the weekend, you might want to spend a bit more time with them.

The point is the workouts I've devised can be done absolutely anywhere and at a time that suits you. You don't need to go to a gym or have had any experience working out in a gym. I demonstrate exactly how to perform each exercise, and they are designed so that you achieve the maximum benefit.

After the 28 days, many of our clients have something of a mental breakthrough. They realise each of the workouts is achievable, the program is sustainable and they've made it a normal part of every day. At the end of the 28 days, we don't encourage them to keep going; they *want* to keep going. Some people are so impressed by the results, they even add a little more exercise to their routines, which is great – what we give you is the foundation, the skeleton, for what you need to do. Anything you add to it is a bonus.

Dear Diary ...

I'm a big believer in making sure that 28 minutes goes into your diary as a priority appointment – one you'd never break. Making that commitment to yourself is absolutely key. Some mums think giving time to themselves is a selfish act and makes them a bad parent, but the opposite is true. If you look after yourself, everyone in your family will benefit. Without a doubt.

Getting started

So many people say to themselves, 'Oh, I'll start on Monday', and just never do. Let's make it easy. Every round of *28 by Sam Wood* starts on the first of the month. And this is what you will need to get yourself started: a smartphone. Yep, that's all.

Each day, a new workout goes online and all you need to do is find that 28 minutes to do it. You can get into it in your office at lunchtime or when your two-year-old is taking a nap. If you travel a lot for work, you can even take it on the road. It actually doesn't matter what time of day you exercise, as long as you do it.

Of course, there are a couple of things that can make the workouts more comfortable (not that they're actually meant to be, but we'll get to that). You could invest in a good pair of running shoes. Particularly as you improve and become fitter, these will become invaluable.

We use light weights in many of our workouts, but, at the start, most people just use milk

The ideal waist

Taking a waist measurement is a very easy way to establish whether you need to work on your health and wellbeing. Carrying extra kilos around the middle can indicate you have excess fat deposits around internal organs like the heart, kidneys and liver. Women who have a waist measurement of greater than 80 centimetres and men who measure more than 94 centimetres around the middle should lose weight to reduce their risk of health problems, including heart disease.

containers (choose either one litre or two, depending on your level) filled with water. They're really easy to hold on to; just make sure you put those lids on tight! At some point, you might want to buy some small two- or three-kilogram dumbbells, but they're not essential.

If you want to you could also buy an exercise mat. If you've got hardwood floors or want to take your workout into the backyard when the weather is nice, it can offer a little padding between you and the ground. Again, only grab one if you think you're going to need it.

Just keep moving

Unless you're at Maniac level, you'll have rest periods between exercises. Especially towards the end of the 28 minutes, if you've been giving it your all, you are going to feel fairly exhausted. So, what should you do during those rest periods? Keep moving. Stand up straight and walk around or on the spot. It helps you get your breath back and stops lactic acid from building up. It's all quite complicated, but that's the stuff that helps you break down glucose into an energy source really quickly. It also then stops muscles from working as efficiently as they should. It's ideal if you're fleeing a threat; not so much if you're working out.

OK, but is this going to hurt?

Pain is relative, but in saying that everything we do at *28 by Sam Wood* is tweaked to fit your lifestyle and level of fitness. We have five levels our clients work through. It starts at Rookie and the top rank is Maniac – of course, there's everything in between as well. The exercises for each level are similar; you simply make your rest periods between movements shorter the fitter you become. Rookies spend 20 seconds working, then 40 seconds resting up for the next exercise. Even if you have never done any exercise or stepped into a gym in your entire adult life, you can have a go at this level. At the other end of the spectrum, our Maniacs work for the entire 60 seconds then go straight into the next movement. In between, the levels add time to the exercise and decrease the fraction of each minute spent in rest mode.

What level you work out is very much a personal thing, and you'll soon be able to tell whether you're going hard enough. If you're a beginner, push yourself until you are quite puffed. If you're more advanced, you'll likely be more attuned to your own capacity. Most of the time, you'll know that your optimum choice is to be working hard enough that it's tough to carry on a conversation, your breathing will be heavy, you'll probably be getting a good sweat on, you'll just be hanging in there and, at the end of the 28 minutes, you'll feel as if you haven't got much left in the tank. If that sounds tough that's because it is, but, believe me, it's also a great feeling.

When you begin, particularly if it's been a while since you last got moving, it is completely normal to feel a bit of muscle soreness in the first week or so. If we do a squat sequence, you might be cursing me as you struggle up the stairs in the next day or two. This is nothing to worry about at all. Those sore muscles are transforming and turning your body into a lean, mean, fat-burning machine. In fact, a little muscle soreness is common even for elite athletes after they've done a tough session.

Any stiffness or aches you feel will be offset by some of the positives you'll see from as early as that first week. Almost immediately you'll find you have more energy – that's from the endorphins (feel-good chemicals) released when you exercise – then, at the end of every day, you'll sleep better too.

It's time to set some goals

It's important to be working towards something concrete, something you can measure. We actively encourage our 28ers to set goals – typically they'll come up with something that's measurable at the end of the 28 days, plus a longer-term target. Always ensure your goals are achievable though; there's nothing more frustrating than following all the rules and still, in your own eyes, falling short.

It may be that you'd ideally like to lose 30 kilograms. That might seem like a lot – and it is – and getting there could seem a long way off. Setting mini goals every month – to lose 4, maybe 5, kilos in each 28-day cycle – won't seem as daunting. When you achieve it, give yourself a high-five and focus on the next month. Before you know it, you'll be three or four months in, you'll have lost 15 kilograms, and already be halfway to your ultimate goal. Plus, I guarantee, you will feel so much better on a day-to-day basis losing the weight will just be an added bonus.

How do you set goals? Well, the first thing is to be true to yourself. Where do you see yourself at the end of the 28 days? After two months? Six months? The good news is that if you're at the point where you know you've got a lot of weight to lose, sticking to the exercise and nutrition program should yield excellent results quickly. Much quicker, say, than someone who leads a fairly active, mainly healthy lifestyle and perhaps needs only to drop those final 5 kilos.

What brings people unstuck time and again is comparing themselves to others. What you're doing is solely about you: your reasons for doing it, your goals, your journey.

Soak it out

If you've been exercising and your muscles have that great ache that lets you know you've been putting in the effort, it's time to reward them. Dissolve some magnesium flakes – available at health-food stores – into a hot bath and just relax. Twenty minutes later, you'll feel the tension, both physical and mental, melt away and you'll sleep like a baby.

For a lot of people, a wellbeing program is mainly about weight loss, and so they become obsessed with the numbers on their bathroom scales. Unfortunately, this can often be more of a hindrance than a help. And here's why ...

From one day to the next, whether or not you've had a perfect run with exercise and nutrition, your weight can fluctuate, mainly due to how much water you've been drinking. (If you doubt this, do an experiment and weigh yourself every few hours during one day. If you've had a few glasses and not been to the loo, you can weigh up to half a kilo more than you did two hours ago.)

What I suggest is that people weigh themselves at the beginning of every 28-day cycle, and that they do it the same way. Every. Single. Time. So, pick a time of day and that's the time you're always going to weigh yourself. If, the first time, you weigh yourself after lunch on the day you've done a workout and you've been to the bathroom three times, then you're going to replicate these same conditions every weighing-in day. You know what's easier though? Get up at your regular time, do a wee, take off whatever you're wearing then jump on the scales (the same set of scales every time).

If you can't hold out till the first of the month, weigh yourself every fortnight. This is the most you should do it though, and you should plan to weigh yourself first thing on every second Monday morning, so you stay accountable over the weekend.

It's true that some people can find scales highly intimidating and a stressful way of measuring progress. Don't worry, because we've got a couple of other suggestions for you. Taking your measurements with a tape measure can work just as well. The fitness industry uses five standard measurements: the waist at the belly button, hips at the widest point, mid-thigh, mid-arm and chest at the nipples. Again, consistency is important, so measure 10 centimetres from the top of your knee cap to find mid-thigh and 8 centimetres from your elbow crease to ensure you're always taking stock of the same place. If it all sounds a bit complicated, the first two measurements are by far the most important for women. For men, the stomach measurement can be a great indicator of progress too.

How you feel and how your clothes fit can tell you how you're getting on, plus there's very little stress or anxiety associated with tracking progress if you use these methods. Of course, you do need to ask yourself if this is going to keep you as accountable as you need to be. Only you'll know that.

We've seen some truly inspirational transformations at *28 by Sam Wood*. People email us with their success stories and will always thank us for showing them the way. We're always touched by those comments, but, really, it was all them. And that's what you need to remember ...

It starts and finishes with you. We give you all the tools you need, then you need to use them. I won't accept the blame if you don't meet your goals, but I won't take the glory either. All you need to do is trust and believe in yourself. You *can* do it.

It pays to be SMART

Telling yourself your goal is to lose weight or be fitter is far too vague – either will set you up for disappointment. SMART is an acronym we use for goal-setting, and it stands for: Specific, Measurable, Accountable, Realistic, Timeframe. If you can plug in the numbers and follow the guidelines, SMART will help you reach your goals. Your first might be to lose three centimetres off your waist in a month. Measure yourself, write the goal down, and make an appointment with yourself to get the tape measure out again in a month. As long as you do the work – that's the accountability part – you'll see results.

But I'm not a morning person

You'll often read research that pinpoints a certain time of day as being the optimum for fat burning, improving your metabolism or some other benefit. Stop reading that stuff! You just need to find 28 minutes a day. It could be first thing in the morning or after the kids go to bed. It doesn't matter. All that matters is that you do it.

The power of positive momentum

'Why every day?' we hear you ask, especially if you've tried a program that encourages rest days throughout the week. Getting into good habits is about exactly that – habits. If you train every day you get into a groove that ultimately becomes self-fulfilling. Train every day, even for 28 minutes, and you'll almost immediately start to feel better and stronger and you'll soon drop a couple of kilograms (if you're trying to lose weight), which makes you want to train more – and on it goes.

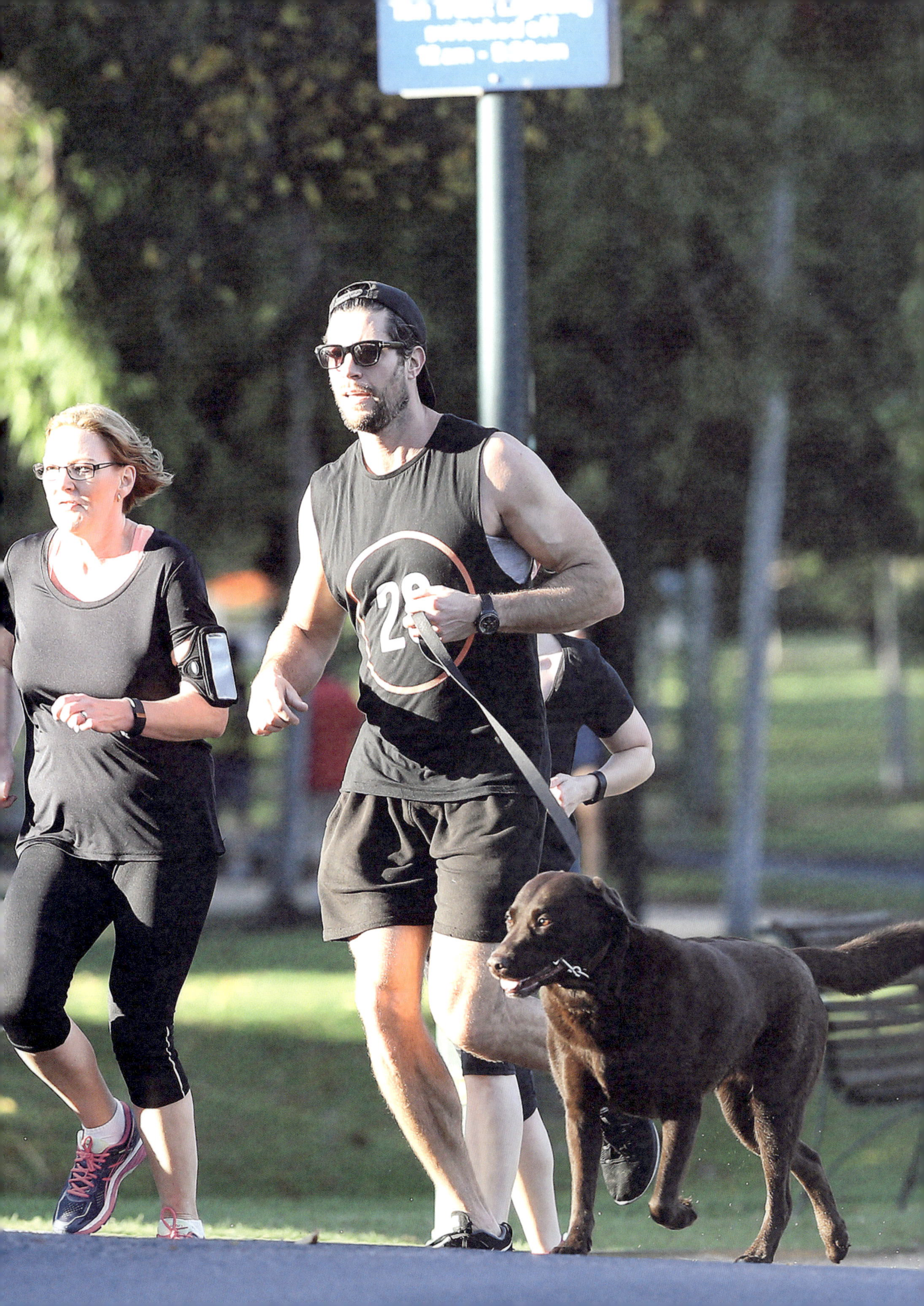

Get your mind right.

Make sleep a habit

Just like making exercise and preparing nutritious food part of your daily routine, setting a schedule for going to bed and waking up will help you get better-quality and more consistent sleep. Crawling into bed then setting the alarm for the same time every day (even on the weekend) helps your body set its own internal clock.

Get your head in the game
Clear your mind and boost your chances of success

We have a saying at 28: 'Life sucks and sings.' It means we need to learn to appreciate and accept that there are things that make us feel on top of the world and events that throw our emotions into chaos. People get caught up in the idea that things should go their way and when they don't it can lead to stress.

Life happens, everything changes and the more we can meet the good and the bad with curiosity and care, the more grounded and open we'll be to what we can learn. We become more ready to drop the myriad small and large complaints and really begin to appreciate the small joys of being alive.

We all know about the amazing psychological and mental benefits of de-stressing, but there is also a correlation between mindfulness and your ability to lose weight. When stress is chronic it causes an increased production of cortisol. High levels of cortisol will lead to your liver dumping glucose into your blood stream, which stops your body's ability to burn fat. If you've been following the program in regards to nutrition and exercise, but you're still not seeing good results, it could be related to chronic stress. If that's the case, some simple mindfulness exercises can help.

Breathe deep, chill out

It can sound very Zen, particularly if you think that getting fit and healthy is all about exercise and eating good nutritious food, but pressing pause on your life for just a few minutes each day can have a radical effect on your stress levels. Yes, we're talking about meditation. Most of us spend our whole lives doing or thinking, but calming your mind for just two to five minutes every day can help your overall wellbeing.

And it's so easy. Whenever you have a moment – you could be standing in line at the supermarket, sitting in traffic or when you first

Soak your troubles away

If you have trouble sleeping, take a hot bath before you head to bed. At night your body temperature naturally starts to slowly drop. Heating it up in the bath makes it cool rapidly immediately after, which is very relaxing.

wake up in the morning – take five deep, slow breaths. Push everything from your mind and concentrate on the rise and fall of your belly, the air filling your lungs right to their deepest pockets, then pushing it all out again. You'll be surprised – especially if you've tried meditation before and found it wasn't for you – at just how easy and effective this method is for clearing your mind.

Visualising a good night's sleep

Many people, especially women, don't get enough shut-eye, so they're not nearly as productive during the day as they could be. It can be difficult to stop the rampage of thoughts that fill your mind as soon as you turn the light out. Even if you do manage to drop off while all that is going on, it can make it harder to slip into the deep, restorative sleep that helps our body and mind efficiently recharge.

Once you're in bed, try this simple exercise. Remember a place that makes you happy and relaxed – it could be the beach, a beautiful forest or even a much-loved room. Once you've got the place in your head, remember everything about it: the colours, textures, what it sounds like and even the people you'd have there with you to make you feel safe. This visualisation should help you relax and drift off to sleep.

Practise gratitude

This is another mindfulness technique that takes only a few minutes, but can make a world of difference, especially if you worry too much. It's even been shown to improve symptoms of depression.

It's as easy as this: at the end of the day, write down three things for which you're grateful. Then write down three amazing things that happened to you during the day. This pushes negative thoughts out of your head and lets you focus on the positive. Occasionally we all have days that are shockers, which can make us feel as though the whole world is ganging up on us. On these days it can be a struggle to recall the good things that happened since you woke up, but even then make yourself do it. Dig deep – it can be as simple a smile from someone you love, cutting into a perfectly ripe avocado, or a short catch-up with a friend. It will remind you that you are safe, everything will be fine and you always have blessings in your life.

Preparing your bedroom for rest

Here are a few simple tips to ensure you're giving yourself the best chance to fall asleep and stay that way the whole night.

* Get rid of any bright lights. They stop your brain from producing melatonin, the hormone that helps you drop off. A dimmer on the main light or a soft lamp will do the trick.

* Don't take electronics into your bedroom. Screens stimulate the mind, so you should stop looking at them at least 30 minutes before you go to bed.

* Make sure your bedroom is dark, quiet, cool and well ventilated. Use blackout curtains as any light from surrounding buildings or the street can interrupt your sleep.

* Keep the notebook you write your gratitude exercises in by your bed and use it before you go to sleep.

* Reading a couple of pages of a novel can also help you turn your mind away from the events of the day (or what might happen tomorrow).

You are what you eat.

Change your habits, change your life.

There are so many rules and theories when it comes to healthy eating. At *28 by Sam Wood* we like to think about turning the traditional food pyramid upside down. We've always been advised to consume diets high in refined carbohydrates and to minimise our intake of fat. However, we now know – and science supports – that our diets should be the opposite when it comes to health and wellness. To keep it simple, we love the acronym JERF. It stands for Just Eat Real Food, which is a simple concept and the most important nutritional goal.

The biggest aim as you're working through your first 28 days – and every 28 days from there on – is to eat food that comes from a tree, out of the ground or from an animal (although, of course, that last option is a personal preference). Where possible, select food with the least human interference, or HI, and avoid, wherever you can, food that comes out of a packet or a box. These are usually the sources of refined carbohydrates – pasta, bread, cereal – and what was the base of the original food pyramid.

To eat healthier, feel better and lose weight, reduce the amount of refined carbohydrates you eat, and focus instead on quality protein and non-starchy vegetables, and partner them with some good fats and wholefood carbohydrates.

While we're talking about turning things upside down, a similar principle can be applied to your plate, too. Because 28 is about progress rather than perfection, we'd never suggest you can't ever have pasta. You do need to turn the ratios upside down though. Keep the portion of pasta small and serve it with larger quantities of quality protein and non-starchy vegetables. That gives you the best of both worlds; you can enjoy pasta (or rice or bread) in moderation but achieve your health and weight-loss goals at the same time.

Eat a healthy breakfast

Getting your day off to a great start can set you up to be much calmer throughout your day. Nutrition is a key factor in your ability to stay calm. With a healthy diet, your body has the nutrition it needs to better regulate your moods. When you are not getting the vitamins and minerals you need, you are more likely to be irritable, which can increase your stress levels throughout the day. Start by eating a nutrient-packed breakfast to boost your energy levels, improve your concentration, and reduce anxiety.

Building your plate

We try to minimise the rules you have to follow at *28 by Sam Wood*, but there are plenty of guidelines that should make your decisions much easier. How you should create a meal is just one of them. You should start with vegetables of the non-starchy variety and ensure you eat the rainbow; choose carrots, capsicum, broccoli, peas, cauliflower and any of your other favourites. These will make up the bulk of your plate, and an ideal goal is to have two cups every meal.

The next thing to add is a palm-sized piece of quality protein. Of course, this can be some sort of meat or fish, but there are other options too. You could choose to have three eggs or half a cup of a plant-based protein source, such as chickpeas, lentils, tofu or tempeh.

Now, you're looking for one portion of good fats. Choose either 30 grams of nuts and seeds, 30 millilitres (about one and a half tablespoons) of olive oil or half an avocado.

Then, and this is optional, you could add one serve – a half to one cup – of a wholefood carbohydrate. These are quinoa, rice, corn and the starchy vegetables, like potato, sweet potato and beetroot.

Whether you're prepping breakfast, lunch or dinner, you can use our plate-building scheme as a guide.

These quality proteins of which you speak...

People are often concerned how much and what sort of meat they should eat. If your personal preference is to live an omnivorous existence, we suggest you eat red meat no more than twice a week. And, where possible, choose grass-raised, since pasture is naturally what cows or sheep would live on. In addition, include chicken and fish in your meals regularly. The most important thing is to get a diversity of food in your diet to maximise the nutrient density of what you eat, introduce your palate to new flavours, and increase your taste preferences.

A big part of *28 by Sam Wood* is meat-free Monday. It's both an important health and environmental decision, so even if not Monday, you should certainly be eating meat-free meals through the week.

It's important for vegetarians and vegans to follow our plate-building guidelines, as it can be easy for them to consume excess carbohydrates. Make sure you include eggs (if you eat them) or plant-based protein with every meal. Some other great protein you should add to your options are nuts and seeds, which double as excellent sources of good fats, and green, leafy vegetables like spinach.

Good fats and bad fats

We started discussing good fats in Build Your Plate. Many are great sources of omega 3, are naturally anti-inflammatory and fantastic for heart health, brain support, mood stabilisation, blood sugar control and satiety. It's so important you include them in the form of olive oil, avocado, nuts and seeds or oily fish at most of your meals.

It may surprise you to learn that certain saturated fats – those that have long been associated with decreased heart health – are no longer demonised. What we've come to learn is that grass-fed butter, coconut cream, milk and oil, and even duck fat are fantastic sources of nutrition with similar health benefits to omega 3s. Research now shows saturated fats do not contribute to chronic illness and the saturated fat–heart health correlation remains one of the biggest nutrition myths of the past five decades. The ingredients we do need to avoid for optimum health and wellness are refined sugars, refined seed oils (canola, sunflower, safflower, cotton seed and the like) and trans fats, which are mainly found in deep-fried foods, margarine and commercially produced cakes and pastries.

When you're cooking, choose good fats for the pan. We suggest cooking with grass-fed butter or coconut oil since both are extremely stable when heated. Olive oil can be used for cooking at low temperatures, preferably under 180°C (350°F), but is much better for cold use, such as in salad dressings. When it becomes too hot, the healthy omega 3s are damaged and can potentially be inflammatory.

Is sugar really that bad?

Well, yes and no. It's important to differentiate between natural sugar – the sort found in fruit – and refined sugar, which makes up all the rest. We shouldn't demonise natural foods, and you should aim to eat two pieces of fruit every day. Try not to consume more than this, as it's still important to control the amount of natural sugars you eat.

The best thing you can do for your health today, however, is to reduce, if not remove, refined sugar from your diet. It sets off the blood sugar rollercoaster, which creates cravings and can give you a severe case of the 'hangrys' (for anyone who hasn't come across this term, it's when you become the vile beast-person who is both hungry and angry, which is terrible for your productivity, food choices, metabolism and relationships). It's the enemy of anyone trying to lose weight because it causes a spike in our fat-storage hormone cortisol. Cortisol is essential in moderate amounts, but if you're already playing havoc with your blood sugar levels by tucking into biscuits, soft drinks and the like, increased cortisol and its glucose conversion will go into overdrive and your body will store fat as a result.

Believe it when you hear that sugar is addictive. Removing or even reducing your consumption can create detoxification symptoms, like intense headaches, tiredness, moodiness and cravings. The good news is this only lasts between four and seven days. If you make positive changes to your nutrition, that is also about the time it takes for your metabolism to switch from burning sugar to burning fat. This fat-burning state is *exactly* what you want to achieve. Think of it as short-term pain for long-term gain.

We always encourage our 28ers to ride out those nasty side effects. You can help yourself by staying hydrated and, if you really feel as if you're going to crumble, having another of our healthy snacks (you'll find a whole chapter of them starting on page 165). If you cave in to your cravings you'll regress and unnecessarily extend the initial adaptation phase.

Speaking of cravings ...

Lots of people talk about cravings for items other than sugar: burgers, chips, pizza and other carbohydrate-laden and salt-heavy foods. It can be good news to learn these cravings are directly related to your previous food choices. The original food pyramid and the associated increased consumption of refined carbohydrates creates poor blood sugar control, with peaks and troughs in energy and the desire to eat even more carbs in an attempt to correct this blood-sugar roller coaster. All of this is very short lived

The truth about good fats

They are really important to your wellbeing for two main reasons. Good fats – from olive and coconut oil, nuts and seeds, avocado – are some of the most nutrient-dense foods you can eat, but they're also our satiety macronutrients. Even a small amount, such as half an avo, will keep your blood sugar levels stable, help stop cravings and make you feel fuller for longer. In short, they're your dietary friends.

and continues the vicious cycle right through 3.30 pm, when 3.30itis hits. It's even better news to learn that 3.30itis is a simple by-product of your previous meals and can be corrected by following our nutritional guidelines.

One of the main strategies to deal with cravings is to start your day right. The food choices you make at breakfast time should closely resemble those you'd make at other meals. Our plate-building guidelines definitely apply at breakfast too, even though, at first, it might seem odd to eat veggies first thing in the morning. Simple examples include tomato, mushrooms and spinach, all of which can easily be added to an omelette or cooked breakfast. Toast can be eaten on occasion, especially if it's sourdough or rye bread.

Throughout the day, if you're starting to feel as though you want to inhale a donut, have a glass of water. Yes, we know it doesn't sound nearly as fun, but thirst is often interpreted as hunger and avoiding dehydration has important health benefits (we'll get to those soon).

That time of the month

It's not uncommon to experience cravings just before the arrival of your period. To help manage this, ensure you consume magnesium-rich foods, such as leafy greens, nuts and seeds, and cacao. Additional magnesium supplementation can also assist. To ensure quality we recommend buying a practitioner-only brand, which is often found behind the counter at your local health-food store. For sweet cravings that you just can't satisfy, try our treat options starting on page 165. Avoiding refined sugar at this time can be quite the challenge, but it is a habit you can practise and become better at each month, especially when you know how much better you feel from making wholefood choices that support your health and wellness goals.

Eating to lose weight, eating to train

Not everyone who joins the *28 by Sam Wood* program is here to lose weight. It is possible to be in the healthy weight range and, at the same time, be lacking in fitness, have low energy levels and feel overly stressed. If you recognise yourself here, this program can absolutely be of a huge benefit to you, too.

There are, however, only two main modifications to make: if you don't need to lose weight, eat a greater volume of food and increase your intake of wholefood carbohydrates. To do this, you can simply add an extra snack per day, or choose to increase the portion sizes of the dishes we've included in the recipe section of *28 by Sam Wood*. Remember our wholefood carbohydrates are quinoa, rice, corn, potato, sweet potato and beetroot, so ensure you select at least one recipe each day with one of these ingredients. In terms of snacks, our Before Training (BT) snacks are higher in carbohydrates, so, if you need to, select one from this list each day.

It's worth remembering, though, even if you're not there yet, that all the weight-loss 28ers eventually move on to our strength meal plans.

Water, water everywhere (and all the other drinks)

The importance of drinking at least 2 litres of water every day cannot be overstated. Hydration is essential for every cellular function, including an efficient metabolism and optimal exercise recovery. When it comes to exercise, we recommend that, for every hour you do, you consume another 500 millilitres. If you're not used to this volume of fluid, you may find you spend half your day going backwards and forwards to the toilet. To minimise this, simply add the juice of half a lemon (our highest electrolyte-containing fruit) or even a pinch of pink or rock salt to help you absorb the water you're drinking and keep you hydrated.

If you find it challenging to drink this volume of water, try some caffeine-free herbal teas and iced teas. Coffee can be consumed, but keep it to two shots a day, or one if you're drinking it with milk, since a latte or cappuccino is a snack.

It's not complicated but ...

Weight loss isn't just a function of calories out being greater than calories in. We must also factor in the influence macronutrients (carbohydrates, protein and fat) have on our physiology. If you eat refined carbs in excess, for example, your insulin levels will spike. Insulin is a hormone that turns carbohydrates into sugar and stores it for future use as, you guessed it, fat.

The fluids you do need to minimise and eventually eliminate are soft drinks and diet soft drinks. We've discussed the health consequences of consuming refined sugar, but, just because they're sugar-free, doesn't mean diet soft drinks are acceptable. Artificial sweeteners have high levels of human interference and are about as far away from JERF as it is possible to get. It's also important to note that anything sweet can lead to poor blood sugar level control and cravings, and keep your palate continuing to crave sweet foods.

Before you go cold turkey though, remember diet soft drinks, particularly those that are caffeinated, can be addictive. When you stop drinking them withdrawal symptoms, similar to when you quit sugar, can occur. What helps is having a plan of attack and to know the cravings will be gone in four to seven days. You may choose to wean yourself off them over the course of a week or two, and substitute with small amounts of green tea, or black tea if you still need a caffeine hit.

The other drink everyone asks us about when they start *28 by Sam Wood* is alcohol. Again, it's not something you have to give up completely, but the more you drink the harder it will be to lose weight. We know that's probably not what you wanted to hear, but it's the reality.

If you're trying to lose weight, we recommend a maximum of two standard drinks a week. Whatever you do avoid sugary cocktails and drinks containing mixers and juices. If you like spirits, choose to drink them mixed with soda water and fresh lime. Dry white or red wine is the lowest sugar choice of the grapes, and it's best to choose a low-carb beer if the amber liquid is your normal choice.

Always ensure you have plenty of alcohol-free days during the week, and, when you are out at the pub or having dinner with friends, have a glass of water or soda water for every alcoholic drink you consume.

I can almost hear what you're thinking: but the Australian guidelines say women can have up to two standard drinks a day (men up to four) with either one or two alcohol-free days each week. Sure, but you are not going shift very much weight if you choose this path. Alcohol interferes with your natural detoxification mechanisms and will encourage your body to store, not burn, fat.

Be truthful: am I going to starve?

The food you'll eat on the *28 by Sam Wood* program is nutrient dense and delicious. We don't count calories and we don't believe in deprivation or restriction, but it is still important to control the amount of food you consume. As such, for the first week or two, as your stomach size adjusts and you begin decreasing your portion sizes, you might feel the odd pang or hear the occasional grumble. It is important to allow your stomach volume to adjust and you'll soon be surprised at how much less you are eating, without hunger, cravings or the blood-sugar roller coaster.

We still give you the option to snack well if you need to, but a big part of changing the way you eat is becoming intuitive and learning to feed your body what it needs. Many of our 28ers only need three meals a day and are continually surprised how satisfying real food can be.

We believe in this program so strongly we guarantee that if you follow it you will never feel hungry again. This is what so many of our 28ers find revolutionary – sometimes, for the first time in years, they're including good fats in their meals, feel full for longer than an hour and are no longer consumed by food, their appetite and their cravings. It really is so simple to follow and, even if you don't know much about nutrition or aren't much of a cook, your life is about to change. So much for the better.

Put knowledge into practice

Now we've given you the basics concerning good food, here's how to make it work.

It's one thing to know and understand the basics of good food, but how can you make it simple? You shouldn't need lots of time – half an hour each evening is all you need to prepare dinner and the next day's lunch – to get your eating in order. Nor do you need to be a Cordon Bleu chef. What you need to remember is that you should enjoy what you eat, and so should the rest of your family. Setting aside some time each week to do the shopping and a little prep is definitely helpful and will help keep you on track.

Here, we've listed the solutions to some of the common questions our *28 by Sam Wood* participants ask. Read through them and you should find that eating well every day becomes a normal way of life.

Is organic better?

We get asked this a lot. It's not necessary to eat entirely organic, but there are certain foods you should aim to buy organic if you can. We (and everyone else concerned with nutrition and the environment) call these the Dirty Dozen, as they're the ones most contaminated by pesticides.

The Dirty Dozen

Apples
Blueberries
Capsicum
Celery
Cucumbers
Grapes
Lettuce
Nectarines
Peaches
Potatoes
Spinach
Strawberries

Buy organic versions of these foods when you can, or at least give them a really good wash when you can't. On the other side of the coin, there are the Clean Fifteen. If buying organic across the board hits your pocket too hard, these could be the exceptions.

The Clean Fifteen

Asparagus	Onions
Avocado	Peas
Cabbage	Pineapples
Eggplant	Rockmelon
Grapefruit	Sweet corn
Kiwifruit	Sweet potato
Mangoes	Watermelon
Mushrooms	

Although we tend to think about fruits and vegetables when it comes to buying organic, the sources of animal protein we choose are also so important. Where possible, look for free range, pasture-fed or grass-fed meat, eggs and milk. It's an important purchasing decision, not only for your own health, but also for the good of the environment. Animals raised this way can roam naturally, are free from added hormones, and produce the correct ratio of good fats. Animals raised in feedlots or fed grain are not environmentally sustainable and also tend to produce higher amounts of omega 6, the inflammatory fatty acid.

Organic meat can definitely be more expensive, especially at your local supermarket. Our favourite cost-saving strategies are buying from a local butcher, purchasing meat in bulk and freezing it, or dealing directly with farmers (try your local farmers' market). Investing in a larger freezer may be an initial expense, but it will save you much time and money in the long run.

Are superfoods really a thing?

Don't get caught up in the hype. Real food is the most nutrient-dense choice you can make, so go down that path whenever you can. In the recipe sections that follow, you'll come across quinoa, goji berries and chia seeds because we're fans of these ingredients – and, in these cases, really healthy ingredients – and show you how easy they are to integrate into meals.

What might surprise my mum?

People are mainly surprised to find that refined carbohydrates aren't nearly as good for us as once thought. Once they were considered the key to health and wellbeing, but as you've already read, real food doesn't come from a box or a packet. At *28 by Sam Wood* we won't tell you not to eat a certain type of food, but swapping supermarket cereals for our breakfast recipes is one of the best decisions you can make.

Get your kitchen sorted

Before you get started on *28 by Sam Wood* it's great to take stock, clean out your pantry, and restock it – and your fridge – with ingredients that will make preparing healthy, nutrient-dense meals easy. We've come up with a list, and while you may not need them all straight away, they will add variety to the types of dishes you can make. Most of what you prepare will be created from the real foods that are the most nutrient dense – fresh veggies, meat, eggs, plant proteins, avocado and the like.

- flours: almond meal, hazelnut meal, coconut flour, buckwheat flour, tapioca flour
- dairy substitutes: unsweetened nut milk, coconut milk, coconut cream, coconut yoghurt

Rice, rice baby

White rice is often criticised in mainstream media because it has a high glycemic index (GI), which causes blood sugar to spike suddenly. What no one takes into account is that you would *never* eat white rice on its own. Once you add it to a curry made with chicken, vegetables and coconut, for example, the GI lowers significantly. Absolutely eat brown rice if you prefer it, but don't think it's healthier or that white rice should be avoided.

- nuts: almonds, hazelnuts, macadamias, cashews, walnuts
- seeds: pepitas, sunflower seeds, chia seeds, tahini
- fats: coconut oil, macadamia oil, olive oil, nut butters, grass-fed butter
- cacao and coconut: cacao powder, cacao nibs, coconut flakes, shredded coconut
- natural sweetness: rice malt syrup, Medjool dates, natvia
- quinoa: quinoa seeds, quinoa flakes
- spices: cinnamon, nutmeg, turmeric, chilli flakes, mixed herbs
- gluten-free baking powder
- sea salt
- eggs
- apple cider vinegar

The banish list

When preparing your pantry and fridge to get started with 28, you'll no longer need these foods and ingredients.

- highly processed cereals and muesli bars, with more than 10 per cent sugar

- anything that says no fat, 97% fat free or fat free on the label – they are normally chock-full of sugar, sweeteners or both
- seed oils, like canola, sunflower and cottonseed
- margarine
- basically if it's not on the JERF list, out it goes!

Can you judge food by its label?

Of course you can. And it's very simple. Always check the sugar content – if there's more than 10 per cent sugar, put it back on the shelf. Ideally, what you're looking for is a label listing fewer than five ingredients, all of which you can pronounce (those ones you can't are best avoided – those high levels of human interference again). Of course, there are exceptions to every rule. If the label lists dates, coconut, almonds and the like and has more than five ingredients that's totally fine – just double check the sugar content.

It's all in the planning

There's one simple way to avoid falling victim to having no food in the fridge and heeding the siren call of takeaway. Get ahead when you have a window of opportunity, and usually that means the weekend. When you're on the *28 by Sam Wood* program, you're sent a menu plan and shopping list on Thursday, so that you can shop on Saturday or Sunday and start to prepare meals for the first half of the week.

Get your lunch for Monday ready on Sunday night and prep a few of your favourite snacks – find them starting on page 165 – so you never get stuck with nothing to eat between meals.

The foundation of the program is using leftovers for lunch. Cooking a double portion in the evening means you can pack away enough for lunch the next day, decreasing both your time in the kitchen and food wastage.

A few other strategies you can utilise include freezing smoothie ingredients in zip-lock bags so you can quickly add them to the blender with water or your choice of milk, and preparing serving sizes of trail mix and veggie sticks to eat with hummus or guacamole.

Use your freezer

If you know you're going to be working late during the week or have to take the kids to a basketball game, it can be a huge advantage to cook meals early in the week and freeze them. Before you leave in the morning put the dish in the fridge to defrost while you're out, and you'll have a meal on the table 10 minutes after you arrive home.

Kitchen equipment

The good news is you don't really need anything special to create our recipes. Just the normal assortment of pots, pans and knives should do the trick. If you want to be really prepared, or try some new ways to prepare meals, you could add these to your cupboard.
- a variety of glass dishes, with lids, in different sizes
- a lunchbox or cooler bag
- a blender
- a food processor
- a spiraliser (these are great because they allow you to turn veggies, like zucchini and carrots, into noodles)
- a lettuce spinner
- a slow cooker is a great investment if you want to prepare meals in advance for freezing

Can I eat out?

Absolutely. Looking after your health doesn't mean you need to cancel your social life. A great tactic is to get online and check a restaurant's menu before you get there. This will ensure there are options that come close to our build-your-plate guidelines and will likely head off any sudden lusting for spaghetti carbonara once you're there.

When you're choosing a cuisine, don't be put off by Indian restaurants. In the past it was thought the dishes served by them were unhealthy because the sauces are often made from coconut or peanuts. The reality is, as long as you don't eat them every night, they can be a really good choice. Choose curries with good protein and lots of vegetables, and have them with a small amount of rice.

In fact, the majority of Asian cuisines can be a good choice, as long as you go for dishes that contain lots of vegetables and avoid ones that have sweet sauces.

Restaurants serving modern Australian dishes will usually have a menu with lots of dishes that fit our build-your-plate guidelines. You could also explore some of the many raw-food cafes that are increasingly popular. They'll be serving smoothies, zucchetti (spaghetti with noodles made from zucchini) and other menu options that are low in carbohydrates and free from refined sugar.

Whenever you're unsure about any sauces or dressings, ask for them to be served on the side or to be replaced with a simple olive oil and lemon juice blend. Get comfortable asking questions and requesting slight modifications to a dish where needed, and you'll never be without options.

You'll definitely be served larger portions than we suggest, but you could order an entree or ask for a doggy bag. It all comes back to becoming an intuitive eater and stopping when you're full.

Sometimes, of course, you may be tempted by dessert. We're all about balance, so why not share one with a friend and try having just one spoonful? It can be (almost) as satisfying as eating the whole plate, but you won't have any of the guilt or cravings the next day. If you can, choose a dessert with good fats, like chocolate and avocado mousse or carrot and walnut cake, rather than sorbet, which is pure frozen sugar.

Do I need to take supplements?

This is dependent on the individual, but you should be getting plenty of nutrients and vitamins if you continue to just eat real food. If you're a vegetarian or vegan and feel you may be lacking in protein, you could add protein powder – choose grass-fed whey protein or a clean pea or hemp protein – to recipes such as smoothies and bliss bites.

Another supplement that can assist with cravings, stress management, recovery from exercise, and menstrual cycle support is magnesium. It's important to choose a practitioner-only brand, often found behind the counter at health-food stores.

Oh no, I ate a whole block of chocolate!

It's not uncommon to fall off the wagon, particularly when you first start the 28 program, but ask yourself this: if you dropped your phone and the screen cracked would you then throw it against the wall?

When it comes to changing your habits it's about what you do every day, not what you do once in a while, that counts.

Chocolate is very high in refined sugar and is designed to make you overeat and become addicted. What you might find when you overindulge is that it can take a couple of days to regain total control, so develop strategies and alternatives to help. If you choose wholefood sweet treats, you'll only need a small amount and they won't start you on that vicious cycle of overeating and the guilt associated with it.

When can I expect to see results?

Everyone is individual, so will see different results in varying time frames. In saying that, you should start to feel the benefits of eating real and getting moving in the first week. To make sure you recognise how your new plan is helping,

Real food

Nature knows best. The best thing you will ever do is minimise your packaged food consumption. Stick with natural nutrition and your body will thank you. Make your number one goal JERF – Just Eat Real Food. Fuel your body with vibrant, colourful, nutrient-rich, real food.
It tastes delicious.

Steph Lowe, Nutritionist

it's important to track energy, how much sleep you're getting, digestion and mood. Write them down in a little notebook – it'll only take you a couple of minutes each day.

In terms of a visible difference, it's often relative to where you're starting from. Someone who makes small changes may experience less-obvious short-term results than someone who has completely overhauled their kitchen and lifestyle.

We encourage people to either track measurements or at least how their clothes are fitting. If you're not seeing the results you'd like, go back to the guidelines. Check, too, if you're snacking too much – sometimes three square meals a day is enough to sustain you. Food diaries can also be helpful to ensure you're not sneaking extra food or drinks that you simply forget about into your days.

If you seem to be doing everything right and it's still not making a difference, check your stress levels. Being constantly worried or on edge can increase the production of cortisol, which can make it difficult to shift weight and particularly stubborn belly fat. Check out our mindset techniques on pages 23 and 24 to get you started.

And don't just think of this as a 28-day program. Most people who start on *28 by Sam Wood* become 28ers for life because the benefits of good nutrition, daily exercise and being mindful are compelling. And addictive.

Recipe key

Diet

GF Gluten Free
V Vegetarian
VE Vegan

Allergy

DF Dairy Free
EF Egg Free
NF Nut Free

Snacks

A General, i.e. can be consumed at any time (Women: up to 2 per day; Men: up to 3 per day).
BT Before Training
AT After Training
T Treat

Note: Lunch and Dinner recipes are interchangeable

28-day meal plan
Week One

DAY 1 - MONDAY

Breakfast	Berry & almond butter smoothie 56
Lunch	Broccoli & kale salad 125
Dinner	Chickpea & pumpkin pilaf 155
Vegetarian recipe alternatives	
Breakfast	Berry & almond butter smoothie 56
Lunch	Broccoli & kale salad 125
Dinner	Chickpea & pumpkin pilaf 155

DAY 2 - TUESDAY

Breakfast	Green eggs & ham 74
Lunch	Leftovers
Dinner	Lamb cutlets with broccoli salad 159
Vegetarian recipe alternatives	
Breakfast	Breakfast salad with fried egg 83
Lunch	Leftovers
Dinner	Creamy vegetable soup 90

DAY 3 - WEDNESDAY

Breakfast	Healthy gut smoothie 85
Lunch	Leftovers
Dinner	Sausages with brussel slaw 160
Vegetarian recipe alternatives	
Breakfast	Healthy gut smoothie 85
Lunch	Leftovers
Dinner	Quinoa, sweet potato & beetroot salad with haloumi 151

DAY 4 - THURSDAY

Breakfast	Tahini granola 73
Lunch	Leftovers
Dinner	Alex's pan-fried salmon with sweet corn & avocado salsa 130
Vegetarian recipe alternatives	
Breakfast	Tahini granola 73
Lunch	Leftovers
Dinner	Mediterranean eggplants with pumpkin & spinach mash 139

DAY 5 - FRIDAY

Breakfast	Snez's kickstarter smoothie 77
Lunch	Raw pad Thai salad with poached chicken 119
Dinner	Coconut fish with sweet potato chips & rocket & tomato salad 143
Vegetarian recipe alternatives	
Breakfast	Snez's kickstarter smoothie 77
Lunch	Raw pad Thai salad with poached chicken 119
Dinner	Walnut & basil zucchetti 101

DAY 6 - SATURDAY

Breakfast	Vegetarian breakfast hash 79
Lunch	Mushroom burger 107
Dinner	Malaysian fish curry with cauliflower rice 148
Vegetarian recipe alternatives	
Breakfast	Vegetarian breakfast hash 79
Lunch	Mushroom burger 107
Dinner	Spicy Mexican bowl with avocado 102

DAY 7 - SUNDAY

Breakfast	Banana & berry pancakes 51
Lunch	Quinoa salad with poached chicken 111
Dinner	Vietnamese prawn rolls with ginger tamari dipping sauce 116
Vegetarian recipe alternatives	
Breakfast	Banana & berry pancakes 51
Lunch	Snez's kale & brussels sprout salad with tahini dressing 93
Dinner	Vietnamese tofu rolls with ginger tamari dipping sauce 116

28-day meal plan Week Two

DAY 8 - MONDAY

Breakfast	Almond & banana chia pudding 55
Lunch	Snez's kale & brussels sprout salad with tahini dressing 93
Dinner	Eggplant parma 138
Vegetarian recipe alternatives	
Breakfast	Almond & banana chia pudding 55
Lunch	Walnut & basil zucchetti 101
Dinner	Chickpea & pumpkin pilaf 155

DAY 9 - TUESDAY

Breakfast	Chocolate for breakfast smoothie 87
Lunch	Leftovers
Dinner	Mexican beef tortillas 140
Vegetarian recipe alternatives	
Breakfast	Chocolate for breakfast smoothie 87
Lunch	Leftovers
Dinner	Pumpkin curry with brown rice 108

DAY 10 - WEDNESDAY

Breakfast	Sautéed greens with eggs & brown rice 80
Lunch	Leftovers
Dinner	Spicy beef burger salad 137
Vegetarian recipe alternatives	
Breakfast	Sautéed greens with eggs & brown rice 80
Lunch	Leftovers
Dinner	Eggplant parma 138

DAY 11 - THURSDAY

Breakfast	Snez's kickstarter smoothie 77
Lunch	Leftovers
Dinner	Steak with pear, broccoli & rocket 156
Vegetarian recipe alternatives	
Breakfast	Snez's kickstarter smoothie 77
Lunch	Leftovers
Dinner	Spicy Mexican bowl with avocado 102

DAY 12 - FRIDAY

Breakfast	Coconut & almond granola with yoghurt & berries 59
Lunch	Pork tenderloin & cauliflower salad 115
Dinner	Mediterranean eggplants with pumpkin & spinach mash 139
Vegetarian recipe alternatives	
Breakfast	Coconut & almond granola with yoghurt & berries 59
Lunch	Tofu san choy bao 112
Dinner	Mediterranean eggplants with pumpkin & spinach mash 139

DAY 13 - SATURDAY

Breakfast	Breakfast salad with fried egg 83
Lunch	Grilled chicken with peach & pistachio salad 94
Dinner	Lamb cutlets with warm broccoli salad 159
Vegetarian recipe alternatives	
Breakfast	Breakfast salad with fried egg 83
Lunch	Snez's kale & brussels sprout salad with tahini dressing 93
Dinner	Tofu san choy bao 112

DAY 14 - SUNDAY

Breakfast	Bacon & egg burritos 48
Lunch	Sweet potato & zucchini fritters with smoked salmon & avocado 105
Dinner	Baked fish with rocket, tomato & tahini 154
Vegetarian recipe alternatives	
Breakfast	Roast vegetable & pesto sandwich 78
Lunch	Sweet potato and zucchini fritters 105
Dinner	Spring vegetable quiche 106

DAY 15 - MONDAY

Breakfast	Green machine smoothie 86
Lunch	Mushroom burger 107
Dinner	Quinoa salad with poached chicken 111
Vegetarian recipe alternatives	
Breakfast	Green machine smoothie 86
Lunch	Mushroom burger 107
Dinner	Creamy vegetable soup 90

DAY 16 - TUESDAY

Breakfast	Peach chia pudding 58
Lunch	Leftovers
Dinner	Baked salmon with zucchini, kale & avocado cashew cream 162
Vegetarian recipe alternatives	
Breakfast	Peach chia pudding 58
Lunch	Leftovers
Dinner	Quinoa, sweet potato & beetroot salad with haloumi 151

DAY 17 - WEDNESDAY

Breakfast	Healthy gut smoothie 85
Lunch	Leftovers
Dinner	Pan-fried chicken with roasted vegetable salad 146
Vegetarian recipe alternatives	
Breakfast	Healthy gut smoothie 85
Lunch	Leftovers
Dinner	Vietnamese tofu rolls with ginger tamari dipping sauce 116

DAY 18 - THURSDAY

Breakfast	Quinoa porridge with cashews & dates 82
Lunch	Prawn salad 97
Dinner	Pork tenderloin & cauliflower salad 115
Vegetarian recipe alternatives	
Breakfast	Quinoa porridge with cashews & dates 82
Lunch	Spicy Mexican bowl with avocado 102
Dinner	Pumpkin curry with brown rice 108

DAY 19 - FRIDAY

Breakfast	Berry breakfast bowl 63
Lunch	Leftovers
Dinner	Eye fillet steak with roasted sweet potato salad 133
Vegetarian recipe alternatives	
Breakfast	Berry breakfast bowl 63
Lunch	Leftovers
Dinner	Tofu san choy bao 112

DAY 20 - SATURDAY

Breakfast	BLD pizza 70
Lunch	Spicy Mexican bowl with avocado 102
Dinner	Baked fish with rocket, tomato & tahini 154
Vegetarian recipe alternatives	
Breakfast	Tahini granola 73
Lunch	Walnut & basil zucchetti 101
Dinner	Chickpea & pumpkin pilaf 155

DAY 21 - SUNDAY

Breakfast	Vegan breakfast salad with guacamole 60
Lunch	Quinoa salad with poached chicken 111
Dinner	Slow-cooked lamb with sautéed greens 152
Vegetarian recipe alternatives	
Breakfast	Vegan breakfast salad with guacamole 60
Lunch	Creamy vegetable soup 90
Dinner	Eggplant parma 138

DAY 25 - THURSDAY

Breakfast	Alex's asparagus & tomato salad with boiled egg 68
Lunch	Leftovers
Dinner	Marinated lamb skewers 144
Vegetarian recipe alternatives	
Breakfast	Alex's asparagus & tomato salad with boiled egg 68
Lunch	Leftovers
Dinner	Spicy Mexican bowl with avocado 102

DAY 22 - MONDAY

Breakfast	Quinoa porridge with banana & walnuts 52
Lunch	Spring vegetable quiche 106
Dinner	Mediterranean eggplants with pumpkin & spinach mash 139
Vegetarian recipe alternatives	
Breakfast	Quinoa porridge with banana & walnuts 52
Lunch	Spring vegetable quiche 106
Dinner	Mediterranean eggplants with pumpkin & spinach mash 139

DAY 26 - FRIDAY

Breakfast	Tahini granola 73
Lunch	Broccoli & kale salad 125
Dinner	Oven baked steak with sweet potato, tomato & spinach 161
Vegetarian recipe alternatives	
Breakfast	Tahini granola 73
Lunch	Broccoli & kale salad 125
Dinner	Raw pad thai salad with tofu 119

DAY 23 - TUESDAY

Breakfast	Smoked salmon omelette 64
Lunch	Leftovers
Dinner	Pan-fried chicken with roasted vegetable salad 146
Vegetarian recipe alternatives	
Breakfast	Sautéed greens with eggs & brown rice 80
Lunch	Leftovers
Dinner	Walnut & basil zucchetti 101

DAY 27 - SATURDAY

Breakfast	Breakfast burrito with avocado 69
Lunch	Greek lamb salad 99
Dinner	Coconut fish & sweet potato chips with rocket & tomato salad 143
Vegetarian recipe alternatives	
Breakfast	Breakfast burrito with avocado 69
Lunch	Snez's kale & brussels sprout salad with tahini dressing 93
Dinner	Eggplant parma 138

DAY 24 - WEDNESDAY

Breakfast	Almond & banana chia pudding 55
Lunch	Leftovers
Dinner	Baked ocean trout on pea mash 147
Vegetarian recipe alternatives	
Breakfast	Almond & banana chia pudding 55
Lunch	Leftovers
Dinner	Chickpea & pumpkin pilaf 155

DAY 28 - SUNDAY

Breakfast	Banana & berry pancakes 51
Lunch	Tuna & quinoa salad with olives 121
Dinner	Steak with pear, broccoli & rocket 156
Vegetarian recipe alternatives	
Breakfast	Banana & berry pancakes 51
Lunch	Roast vegetable & pesto sandwich 78
Dinner	Quinoa, sweet potato & beetroot salad with haloumi 151

Breakfast.

Your mum says it's the most important meal of the day and she's right. Not just tasty, these breakfasts will also make you feel fuller for longer and get your day off to a nutritious start.

Bacon & egg burritos

Serves 2 | Preparation time: 5 minutes | Cooking time: 5 minutes

2 bacon rashers

2 eggs

8 cherry tomatoes, halved

¼ small onion, chopped

2 corn tortilla wraps

2 tablespoons Greek-style yoghurt

1 tablespoon dijon mustard

100 g (3½ oz/2 cups) baby spinach leaves

2 tablespoons finely chopped coriander (cilantro) leaves

sea salt and freshly ground black pepper

Breakfast burritos? Now you're talking! While these may feel like a massive treat, so long as you use grass-fed, pasture-raised bacon they also offer up the perfect balance of protein and healthy fats – giving you the slow, steady release of energy you need to get your day started in just the right way.

In a non-stick frying pan, dry-fry the bacon over a medium heat for 5–6 minutes until golden and crispy, then remove from the pan with a spatula and set aside on paper towel to drain.

Whisk together the eggs, cherry tomatoes and onion in a large bowl. Pour the egg mixture into the pan and cook for 2 minutes, or until just set, then flip with a spatula and cook for a further 1–2 minutes. Remove from the pan and cut in half.

To serve, divide the tortilla wraps between serving plates and spread with the yoghurt and mustard. Lay over the crispy bacon rashers and omelette halves, then top with the spinach leaves and coriander. Season and serve immediately.

nutritional info:
Energy 1198 kj
Calories 287 cal
Protein 15 g
Fibre 2 g
Fat 14 g
Saturated Fat 5 g
Carbs 23 g
Sugar 5 g

GF | NF

Banana & berry pancakes

Serves 1 | Preparation time: 5 minutes | Cooking time: 10 minutes

2 eggs

¼ teaspoon gluten-free baking powder

½ teaspoon ground cinnamon

1 tablespoon coconut flour

½ large banana, mashed

1 teaspoon coconut oil

2 tablespoons plain yoghurt

60 g (2 oz/½ cup) fresh raspberries

Berries are my favourite fruit: they are low in sugar and rich in antioxidants, vitamin C and several B vitamins. We also love bananas because they are one of the best natural sources of carbohydrates. Just be mindful that they are a higher-sugar fruit and stick to half a banana.

Add the eggs, baking powder, cinnamon and coconut flour to a mixing bowl and whisk to form a light batter. Add the banana and mix together to combine, adding a splash of water if the batter is too thick.

Melt the coconut oil in a small frying pan over a medium heat, then add a quarter of the pancake batter and tilt the pan to cover the base evenly. Cook for 2–3 minutes until small bubbles appear on the top of the pancake, then gently flip over and cook for a further 2–3 minutes. Remove from the pan and keep warm, then repeat with the remaining pancake mixture.

To serve, pile the pancakes onto a plate as a rough stack, dollop over the yoghurt and scatter over the raspberries to finish.

nutritional info:
Energy 1281 kj
Calories 305 cal
Protein 16 g
Fibre 6 g
Fat 16 g
Saturated Fat 8 g
Carbs 25 g
Sugar 12 g

GF | V | NF

Quinoa porridge with banana & walnuts

Serves 2 | **Preparation time: 5 minutes** | **Cooking time: 15 minutes**

250 ml (8½ fl oz/1 cup) almond milk, plus extra if necessary

100 g (3½ oz/½ cup) quinoa, rinsed

1 teaspoon rice malt syrup

1 tablespoon frozen blueberries

½ small banana, sliced

1 tablespoon roughly chopped walnuts

One of my favourite sources of carbohydrate, quinoa also has a super-high protein content, making it a perfect source of nutrition for vegetarians and vegans. I like to double the quantity I need when making this, freezing the second portion for next time or enjoying it as a snack later in the week.

Heat two-thirds of the almond milk in a saucepan over a medium heat until warm, then add the quinoa, stirring well. Bring to a simmer and cook for about 15 minutes, stirring, or until all the liquid has been absorbed.

Remove the porridge from the heat and stir in the rice malt syrup and blueberries, then divide between bowls. Scatter over the banana slices and chopped walnuts and pour an extra 2–3 tablespoons almond milk over each bowl if you prefer a thinner consistency for your porridge. Serve.

nutritional info:
Energy 1517 kj
Calories 363 cal
Protein 8 g
Fibre 7 g
Fat 14 g
Saturated Fat 1 g
Carbs 44 g
Sugar 12 g

GF | V | DF | EF

Almond & banana chia pudding

Serves 1 | Preparation time: 30 minutes plus soaking

2 tablespoons chia seeds

3 tablespoons coconut milk

1 vanilla bean, split lengthways and seeds scraped

1½ teaspoons rice malt syrup

½ banana, thinly sliced on the diagonal

2 tablespoons roughly chopped almonds

pinch of ground cinnamon

I love chia puddings as they provide the perfect nutrient-dense alternative to breakfast cereal. The touch of sweetness here comes from the rice malt syrup – a natural fructose-free sweetener that won't give your blood sugar levels that same crazy spike (and then crash) as highly processed sugars.

Place the chia seeds, coconut milk, vanilla seeds, 1 teaspoon of the rice malt syrup and 100 ml (3½ fl oz) water in an airtight container and leave to soak overnight in the refrigerator.

To serve, spoon the chia mixture into a glass or bowl and top with the banana slices and chopped almonds. Drizzle over the remaining rice malt syrup and sprinkle over the cinnamon to finish.

nutritional info:
Energy 1710 kj
Calories 409 cal
Protein 11 g
Fibre 13 g
Fat 29 g
Saturated Fat 10 g
Carbs 21 g
Sugar 14 g

V | VE | GF | EF | DF

Berry & almond butter smoothie

Serves 1 | Preparation time: 2 minutes

165 g (6 oz/¾ cup) mixed berries, fresh or frozen

60 g (2 oz/¼ cup) plain yoghurt

250 ml (8½ fl oz/1 cup) unsweetened almond milk

1 heaped tablespoon desiccated (shredded) coconut

1 tablespoon almond butter

Smoothies are such a speedy, delicious way to start your day – perfect for when you need to get out the door and get on with things as quickly as possible. Filled with antioxidants and natural carbohydrates, this particular one's a winner.

Place all of the ingredients in a blender or food processor and whiz everything together until smooth. Pour into a glass and enjoy.

Note: These smoothies are decorated using almond butter and shaved coconut – which will tip the nutritionals!

G | GF | V | EF

nutritional info:
Energy 1293 kj
Calories 309 cal
Protein 7 g
Fibre 2 g
Fat 16 g
Saturated Fat 8 g
Carbs 32 g
Sugar 24 g

Peach chia pudding

Serves 2 | Preparation time: 15 minutes plus soaking | Cooking time: 12 minutes

60 g (2 oz/½ cup) chia seeds

1 vanilla bean, seeds scraped

1 tablespoon rice malt syrup

400 ml (13½ fl oz) coconut milk, unsweetened

2 large peaches

juice of ½ lemon

1 tablespoon rice malt syrup

½ teaspoon ground cinnamon

GF | V | VE | DF | EF | NF

Add the chia seeds to a bowl together with the vanilla seeds and rice malt syrup. Pour over the coconut milk and stir together well, then transfer to the refrigerator and leave to soak overnight.

The next day, peel and dice the peaches. Place the peaches, lemon juice and rice malt syrup in a saucepan over a high heat and bring to the boil. Reduce the heat to a simmer and cook for 12 minutes or until the peaches are tender. Add the cinnamon and mash the peaches roughly with a fork. Set aside to cool slightly.

To serve, divide the chia pudding between bowls, spoon over the mashed peaches and stir gently to combine. Enjoy.

nutritional info:
Energy 1485 kj
Calories 355 cal
Protein 13 g
Fibre 26 g
Fat 16 g
Saturated Fat 5 g
Carbs 41 g
Sugar 11 g

Berry coconut chia pudding

Serves 2 | Preparation time: 15 minutes plus soaking

3 tablespoons chia seeds

250 ml (8½ fl oz/1 cup) almond milk

1 teaspoon rice malt syrup

1 teaspoon vanilla extract

2 tablespoons chopped almonds

155 g (5½ oz/1 cup) blueberries

3 tablespoons coconut flakes

GF | V | VE | DF | EF

Place the chia seeds, almond milk, rice malt syrup, vanilla extract, almonds and half the blueberries in an airtight container and stir well to combine. Transfer to the fridge and leave to soak overnight.

To serve, divide the chia pudding between bowls and top with the coconut flakes, remaining blueberries and, if you like things sweeter, an extra teaspoon of rice malt syrup.

nutritional info:
Energy 1339 kj
Calories 320 cal
Protein 9 g
Fibre 13 g
Fat 18 g
Saturated Fat 6 g
Carbs 32 g
Sugar 14 g

Coconut & almond granola with yoghurt & berries

Serves 12 | **Preparation time: 3 minutes** | **Cooking time: 15 minutes**

110 g (4 oz/2 cups) coconut flakes

155 g (5½ oz/1 cup) almonds, roughly chopped

30 g (1 oz/¼ cup) pepitas (pumpkin seeds)

40 g (1½ oz/¼ cup) sunflower kernels

2 tablespoons chia seeds

1 tablespoon ground cinnamon

60 ml (2 fl oz/¼ cup) coconut oil, melted

2 tablespoons rice malt syrup

TO SERVE (PER PERSON)

100 g (3½ oz) Greek-style yoghurt

60 g (2 oz/½ cup) fresh raspberries

Preheat the oven to 180°C (350°F) and line a baking tray with baking paper.

Add all the ingredients to a large bowl and mix together thoroughly to ensure the coconut flakes, almonds and seeds are evenly coated in the coconut oil and rice syrup.

Spread the granola over the baking tray in an even layer and bake for 10–15 minutes, checking regularly and stirring from time to time, until golden brown and evenly cooked.

Remove from the oven and leave to cool, then transfer to a suitable airtight container and store for up to 2 weeks. To serve, top with yoghurt and fresh raspberries.

nutritional info:
Energy 1456 kj
Calories 348 cal
Protein 8 g
Fibre 12 g
Fat 27 g
Saturated Fat 17 g
Carbs 24 g
Sugar 6 g

GF | V | EF

Vegan breakfast salad with guacamole

Serves 1 | Preparation time: 10 minutes | Cooking time: 2–3 minutes

½ teaspoon coconut oil

2 tablespoons pepitas (pumpkin seeds)

½ broccoli head, broken into florets and diced

large handful of mixed lettuce leaves

1 large tomato, diced

1 tablespoon kimchi

juice of 1 lemon

sea salt and freshly ground black pepper

GUACAMOLE

½ avocado

½ tomato, chopped

4 tablespoons chopped coriander (cilantro) leaves and stalks

½ red onion, chopped

juice of 1 lemon

1 teaspoon sea salt

This is such a simple and tasty breakfast salad that it will no doubt make the leap over to lunch and dinner too. The home-made guacamole here is a great one to have in your kitchen repertoire – it's perfect for stirring by the spoonful into salad dressings or for enjoying as a snack with vegetable sticks for dipping.

Melt the coconut oil in a small frying pan over a medium heat, add the pepitas and toast for 2–3 minutes until lightly golden. Remove from the pan and set aside.

Bring a small saucepan of water to the boil, add the broccoli and blanch for 3–4 minutes, or until just tender. Drain and set aside to cool.

To make the guacamole, add all the ingredients to a food processor and pulse together to your desired consistency.

Once cool, add the broccoli to a large serving bowl together with the lettuce leaves, tomato, kimchi and toasted pepitas. Toss together well and squeeze over the lemon juice, then season with salt and pepper and dollop over the guacamole to finish. Enjoy.

GF | V | DF | EF | NF

nutritional info:
Energy 1519 kj
Calories 363 cal
Protein 23 g
Fibre 11 g
Fat 26 g
Saturated Fat 8 g
Carbs 28 g
Sugar 7 g

Berry breakfast bowl

Serves 1 | Preparation time: 5 minutes

60 g (2 oz/½ cup) frozen raspberries

80 g (2¾ oz/½ cup) frozen blueberries

1 teaspoon almond butter or other nut butter

large handful of baby spinach leaves

1 tablespoon chia seeds

¼ teaspoon ground cinnamon

250 ml (8½ fl oz/1 cup) almond milk or other nut milk

TO SERVE

1 teaspoon coconut flakes

1 teaspoon cacao nibs

1 teaspoon goji berries

Goji berries are a great source of antioxidants, and they stand apart from other berries because they are extremely high in essential amino acids (protein), fatty acids and beta-carotene, which is great for your skin.

Place all the ingredients into a high-speed blender or food processor and blend until thick and creamy (if the consistency is a little too thick, add a little extra almond milk).

To serve, spoon into a bowl and sprinkle over the coconut flakes, cacao nibs and goji berries in neat lines to finish. Enjoy.

Note: If you use more coconut flakes, cacao nibs and goji berries than the recipe, the nutritionals will change.

nutritional info:
Energy 1272 kj
Calories 304 cal
Protein 8 g
Fibre 17 g
Fat 16 g
Saturated Fat 1 g
Carbs 39 g
Sugar 16 g

GF | V | VE | DF | EF

Smoked salmon omelette

Serves 1 | Preparation time: 5 minutes | Cooking time: 6 minutes

¼ teaspoon olive oil

2 eggs, beaten

1 spring onion (scallion), finely sliced

2 asparagus spears, trimmed and roughly chopped

50 g (1¾ oz) smoked salmon, torn into flakes

sea salt and freshly ground black pepper

handful of rocket (arugula)

Smoked salmon is a fantastic protein source, rich in healthy omega 3 fats. The combination of protein and good fats provides blood sugar control, satiety, exercise recovery and a metabolism geared to burning fat for fuel.

Preheat the grill (broiler) to high.

Heat the oil in a small frying pan over a medium heat. Pour in the beaten egg and tilt the pan so it covers the base, then scatter over the spring onion, asparagus and smoked salmon pieces. Season generously with salt and pepper and cook for 3 minutes, then place the pan under the grill and cook for a further 3 minutes, or until the omelette is lightly browned and cooked to your liking.

To serve, slide the omelette onto a plate and top with the rocket leaves.

GF | DF | NF

nutritional info:
**Energy 1230 kj
Calories 294 cal
Protein 33 g
Fibre 2 g
Fat 19 g
Saturated Fat 4 g
Carbs 10 g
Sugar 7 g**

Chorizo hash

Serves 1 | Preparation time: 15 minutes | Cooking time: 10 minutes

75 g (2¾ oz/½ cup) pumpkin (winter squash), peeled and chopped into 2 cm (¾ in) cubes

10 g (¼ oz) salted butter

100 g (3½ oz) cooking chorizo, chopped

1 bacon rasher, chopped

1 zucchini (courgette), finely diced

½ broccoli head, broken into small florets

2 handfuls of baby spinach leaves

½ avocado, chopped

lemon wedges, to serve

Chorizo and bacon together? Yes please! Gone are the days of fearing fat, especially when quality is prioritised. Cured meats are still considered a sometimes food, but I want you to be able to achieve your health and wellness goals with enjoyment, not deprivation.

Add the pumpkin to a steamer set over simmering water and steam for 5–10 minutes, or until just tender. Set aside.

Melt the butter in a large frying pan over a medium heat, add the steamed pumpkin, chorizo and bacon and sauté for 4–5 minutes until browned. Add the zucchini and broccoli and cook, stirring, for 1–2 minutes or until slightly softened, then stir in the spinach leaves and mix everything together well.

To serve, spoon the hash into a serving bowl, top with the avocado and enjoy with lemon wedges for squeezing.

nutritional info:
Energy 1491 kj
Calories 356 cal
Protein 17 g
Fibre 6 g
Fat 28 g
Saturated Fat 10 g
Carbs 6 g
Sugar 5 g

GF | NF | EF

Alex's asparagus & tomato salad with boiled egg

Serves 1 | Preparation time: 5 minutes | Cooking time: 10 minutes

80 g (2¾ oz/½ cup) peas, fresh or frozen

1 egg

200 g (7 oz) baby asparagus, trimmed

125 g (4½ oz) cherry tomatoes, halved

handful of baby spinach leaves

½ avocado, sliced

DRESSING

2 teaspoons olive oil

1 teaspoon lemon juice

1 teaspoon finely chopped chives

pinch of sea salt

pinch of freshly ground black pepper

This is one of my brother Alex's favourite breakfasts. I love the combo of charred tender asparagus, juicy cherry tomatoes and creamy avocado – who says you can't start the day with veg?

Add the peas to a saucepan of boiling water and cook for 2–3 minutes, until the peas are tender. Drain and set aside.

Place the egg in a small saucepan and cover with cold water. Bring to the boil, then reduce the heat to medium and simmer gently for 5–7 minutes, or until cooked to your liking. Remove from the pan and leave to cool, then peel and set aside.

Meanwhile, heat a non-stick frying pan over a medium heat, add the asparagus and dry-fry for 2–3 minutes, stirring, or until just tender. Set aside to cool.

To make the dressing, mix all the ingredients together in a small bowl.

Once cool, add the asparagus to a mixing bowl together with the tomatoes, spinach and peas. Pour over the dressing and mix together well, then transfer to an individual serving plate or bowl.

To serve, slice the boiled egg and use to top the salad along with the avocado.

nutritional info:
Energy 1633 kj
Calories 390 cal
Protein 12 g
Fibre 10 g
Fat 32 g
Saturated Fat 7 g
Carbs 8 g
Sugar 6 g

G | V | GF | NF | DF

Breakfast burrito with avocado

Serves 1 | Preparation time: 5 minutes | Cooking time: 5 minutes

2 eggs

1 teaspoon finely chopped chives

sea salt and freshly ground black pepper

½ teaspoon olive oil

1 small corn tortilla

handful of baby spinach leaves

¼ avocado, mashed

I love this simple, warm burrito filled with creamy scrambled egg and avocado. If you have one, try popping it in a sandwich press and giving it a light toasting before serving for a little extra crunch.

Preheat the oven to 100°C (210°F).

Whisk together the eggs and chives in a small bowl. Season.

Heat the oil in a small frying pan over a medium heat. Add the egg mixture and cook for 2–3 minutes, stirring gently with a wooden spoon and gently pushing the mixture in from edges, until the eggs are just scrambled.

Meanwhile, transfer the tortilla to the oven for 2 minutes to warm.

To serve, place the warm tortilla on a serving plate and top with the spinach, scrambled egg and avocado. Season generously with salt and pepper, then wrap and enjoy.

nutritional info:
Energy 1167 kj
Calories 279 cal
Protein 15 g
Fibre 5 g
Fat 18 g
Saturated Fat 4 g
Carbs 15 g
Sugar 2 g

GF | V | DF | NF

BLD pizza

Serves 2 | Preparation time: 10 minutes | Cooking time: 20 minutes

2 wholegrain or gluten-free pitta wraps

2 tablespoons tomato paste (concentrated purée)

8 cherry tomatoes, halved

20 g (¾ oz) feta, crumbled

50 g (1¾ oz) ham, roughly chopped

2 eggs

1 teaspoon dried or fresh thyme leaves

2 handfuls of rocket (arugula)

sea salt and freshly ground black pepper

I call this my 'BLD' pizza as I think it's perfect for breakfast, lunch or dinner. Pizza for breakfast? Well, so long as you use good, healthy produce like this I don't see that there's any reason you shouldn't both grab a morning slice and achieve your wellness goals. So go on, get stuck in!

Preheat the oven to 180°C (350°F) and line a baking tray with baking paper.

Lay the pitta wraps on the tray, spread over the tomato paste and top with the cherry tomatoes, feta and ham. Crack an egg over the centre of each pizza, then scatter over the thyme and bake in the oven for 10–15 minutes, or until the egg is cooked to your liking.

Remove from the oven, top with the rocket and season with salt and pepper. Cut into slices to serve.

GF | NF

nutritional info:
Energy 1319 kj
Calories 314 cal
Protein 18 g
Fibre 3 g
Fat 10 g
Saturated Fat 4 g
Carbs 38 g
Sugar 7 g

Tahini granola

Serves 10 | Preparation time: 10 minutes | Cooking time: 20 minutes

100 g (3½ oz/1 cup) rolled (porridge) oats or quinoa flakes (for gluten-free)

55 g (2 oz/1 cup) coconut flakes

30 g (1 oz/¼ cup) pepitas (pumpkin seeds)

60 g (2 oz/½ cup) chopped pecans

1 tablespoon ground cinnamon

½ teaspoon sea salt

60 ml (2 fl oz/¼ cup) maple syrup

65 g (2¼ oz/¼ cup) tahini

1 teaspoon vanilla extract

TO SERVE (PER PERSON):

50 g (1¾ oz) Greek-style yoghurt

50 g (1¾ oz/⅓ cup) fresh blueberries

If your household is anything like ours, this tahini granola will soon become a firm family favourite – in fact, the real challenge will be restricting yourselves to just one portion each a day! Making the granola up in a big batch like this means you'll always have a healthy option on hand to start your day the right way.

Preheat the oven to 160°C (320°F). Line a baking tray with baking paper.

Add the oats, coconut flakes, pepitas, pecans, cinnamon and salt to a large bowl and mix together well.

In a separate bowl, mix together the maple syrup, tahini and vanilla. Pour the syrup mixture over the dry ingredients and stir well to coat evenly.

Spread the granola over the prepared baking tray in an even layer and bake for 15–20 minutes, stirring and turning the ingredients halfway through cooking, until golden brown and evenly cooked.

Remove from the oven and leave to cool, then transfer to an airtight jar and store for up to 2 weeks. To serve, top with yoghurt and fresh blueberries.

nutritional info:
Energy 1296 kj
Calories 310 cal
Protein 8 g
Fibre 3 g
Fat 20 g
Saturated Fat 8 g
Carbs 25 g
Sugar 15 g

V | EF

Green eggs & ham

Serves 4 | Preparation time: 25 minutes | Cooking time: 5 minutes

100 g (3½ oz/½ cup) multi-coloured quinoa, rinsed

155 g (5½ oz/1 cup) peas

200 g (7 oz) asparagus, trimmed and halved

1 tablespoon apple cider vinegar

4 eggs

2 tablespoons roughly chopped basil

2 tablespoons roughly chopped almonds

4 prosciutto slices

30 g (1 oz) goat's feta, crumbled

sea salt and freshly ground black pepper

This is my favourite recipe, and not just because it's referred to as Green Eggs and Sam in the 28 kitchen! It also tastes great – the combo of lightly steamed peas and asparagus with the salty prosciutto and feta delivers up a winning mix of fresh and savoury flavours.

Bring 250 ml (8½ fl oz/1 cup) water to the boil in a saucepan, add the quinoa, cover with a lid and cook for 15 minutes, fluffing up the grains halfway through cooking with a fork for extra volume, until the grains are tender and the water has been absorbed. Set aside to cool.

Meanwhile, add the peas and asparagus to a steamer set over simmering water and steam for 3–4 minutes, or until just tender. Set aside.

Add the apple cider vinegar to a small saucepan of boiling water and reduce to a simmer. Crack the eggs into separate cups and stir the water clockwise to create a gentle whirlpool, then carefully tip the eggs into the swirling water and cook for 3 minutes, or until the whites have completely cooked. Remove with a slotted spoon and drain on paper towel.

Add the cooked quinoa, peas and asparagus to a large bowl together with the basil and almonds and mix well. Divide among serving plates, top with the prosciutto and poached eggs and scatter over the goat's feta. Season generously with salt and pepper and enjoy.

nutritional info:
Energy 1121 kj
Calories 268 cal
Protein 22 g
Fibre 5 g
Fat 15 g
Saturated Fat 4 g
Carbs 15 g
Sugar 4 g

GF

Snez's kickstarter smoothie

Serves 1 | Preparation time: 2 minutes

375 ml (12½ fl oz/1½ cups) almond milk

1 x 30 ml (1 fl oz) shot cold-drip or espresso coffee

1 banana

1 tablespoon rolled (porridge) oats

1 teaspoon chia seeds

1 teaspoon honey

This is Snez's favourite smoothie and one of the most popular brekkie options on my 28 program. To make it gluten free, simply switch the oats for brown rice flakes or quinoa flakes.

Place all of the ingredients in a high-speed blender or food processor and whiz everything together for about 1 minute, or until smooth. Pour into a glass and enjoy.

nutritional info:
Energy 1390 kj
Calories 332 cal
Protein 7 g
Fibre 7 g
Fat 14 g
Saturated Fat 1 g
Carbs 42 g
Sugar 24 g

V | DF | EF

Roast vegetable & pesto sandwich

Serves 1 | **Preparation time: 5 minutes** | **Cooking time: 20 minutes**

½ red capsicum (bell pepper), seeds removed

2 x 2 cm (¾ in) eggplant (aubergine) slices

1½ teaspoons olive oil

1½ teaspoons good-quality basil pesto

2 slices wholegrain or gluten-free bread

1 small handful of rocket (arugula)

I love getting veggies into my breakfasts where I can, as this sandwich shows. I like to make the roasted veg in advance and then it's just a quick assembly job needed to turn this into a speedy breakfast-on-the-go. For something special, try it toasted in a sandwich press or on a hot grill plate just before serving.

Preheat the oven to 180°C (350°F).

Arrange the capsicum and eggplant slices on a baking tray and brush with the olive oil. Roast in the oven for 20–25 minutes, or until softened. Set the roasted vegetables aside to cool, placing the capsicum in a bowl covered with plastic wrap. Once cool, remove the plastic wrap and scrape the skin off the capsicum with a teaspoon.

When ready to eat, spread the basil pesto evenly over a slice of bread. Pile over the eggplant, capsicum and rocket and finish with the remaining bread slice. Cut in half and enjoy.

nutritional info:
Energy 1418 kj
Calories 339 cal
Protein 10 g
Fibre 10 g
Fat 13 g
Saturated Fat 2 g
Carbs 45 g
Sugar 9 g

GF | V | EF

Vegetarian breakfast hash

Serves 1 | Preparation time: 5 minutes | Cooking time: 10 minutes

65 g (2¼ oz) potato, cut into 1 cm (½ in) cubes

10 g (¼ oz) salted butter

1 green capsicum (bell pepper), finely diced

3 asparagus spears, trimmed and finely diced

50 g (1¾ oz) kale, stems removed and leaves finely diced

1 egg

15 g (½ oz) goat's feta, crumbled

1 tablespoon kimchi

You have probably worked out by now that veggies for breakfast is a thing at 28. Sure, it might be less conventional than toast or cereal but increasing the nutrient density of your first meal of the day will control your blood sugar, cravings, mood and ongoing satiety.

Add the potato to a steamer set over simmering water and steam for 5–6 minutes, or until just tender.

Heat the butter in a large frying pan over a medium heat, add the steamed potato and sauté for 4–5 minutes until caramelised. Add the capsicum, asparagus and kale and cook, stirring, for 1–2 minutes or until slightly softened.

Using a spoon, make an indentation in the vegetable mixture, then crack the egg into it. Cook for 3 minutes until the egg whites are firm and the yolks have only just set, or for a little longer if you prefer your eggs well cooked.

To serve, spoon the hash into a serving bowl, top with the feta and kimchi and enjoy.

nutritional info:
Energy 1619 kj
Calories 387 cal
Protein 15 g
Fibre 5 g
Fat 17 g
Saturated Fat 9 g
Carbs 41 g
Sugar 3 g

GF | V | NF

Sautéed greens with eggs & brown rice

Serves 2 | Preparation time: 10 minutes | Cooking time: 25 minutes

65 g (2¼ oz/⅓ cup) brown rice

4 eggs

30 g (1 oz) salted butter

1 brown onion, finely chopped

2 garlic cloves, finely chopped

1 zucchini (courgette), chopped

1 broccoli head, florets chopped

155 g (5½ oz/1 cup) peas, fresh or frozen

125 ml (4 fl oz/½ cup) vegetable stock

100 g (3½ oz/2 cups) baby spinach leaves

30 g (1 oz) goat's feta

While brown rice for breakfast might not normally be your thing, I urge you to give it a try, especially if you find yourself prone to the mid-morning snacks. The natural carbohydrates and fibre it contains – along with the protein and good fats found in the eggs here – will help keep you nicely satisfied through to lunch.

Add the rice to a saucepan, cover with 170 ml (5½ fl oz/⅔ cup) water and bring to a boil. Cover with a lid, reduce the heat to a simmer and cook for 25 minutes. Drain off any remaining water and rinse the rice under cool water. Set aside until needed.

While the rice is cooking, place the eggs in a small saucepan and cover with cold water. Bring to the boil, then reduce the heat to medium and simmer gently for 5–7 minutes, or until cooked to your liking. Remove from the pan and leave to cool, then peel and set aside.

Melt the butter in a saucepan over a medium–high heat, add the onion and garlic and cook for 5–6 minutes, or until the onion has softened and browned. Add the zucchini, broccoli and peas to the pan and cook, stirring, for 2 minutes, then lower the heat, pour over the vegetable stock and cook for a further 4–5 minutes, or until the vegetables are nice and tender. Stir in the spinach and cooked brown rice, then remove from the heat and divide between bowls.

To serve, slice the boiled eggs and use to top the sautéed greens along with the goat's feta.

nutritional info:
Energy 1657 kj
Calories 396 cal
Protein 20 g
Fibre 9 g
Fat 21 g
Saturated Fat 11 g
Carbs 35 g
Sugar 8 g

GF | V | NF

Quinoa porridge with cashews & dates

Serves 2 | Preparation time: 10 minutes plus soaking | Cooking time: 15 minutes

65 g (2¼ oz/⅓ cup) quinoa

pinch of sea salt

250 ml (8½ fl oz/1 cup) almond milk

1 teaspoon vanilla extract

1 teaspoon ground cinnamon

1 small handful of cashews, finely chopped

1 medjool date, pitted and finely chopped

¼ banana, diced

1 teaspoon rice malt syrup

This super tasty take on traditional porridge provides the perfect start to your day, especially when it's cold outside. The combination of rice malt syrup, date and banana delivers all the delicious natural sweetness you need, while the quinoa is an excellent source of both carbohydrate and protein.

Put the quinoa in a bowl, cover with water and leave to soak for 10 minutes. Drain and rinse under cold running water.

Add 250 ml (8½ fl oz/1 cup) water to a saucepan with the salt. Bring to the boil, add the quinoa and reduce to a simmer, then cover with a lid and cook for 10 minutes, or until all the water has been absorbed.

Remove the lid from the pan, add the almond milk, vanilla, cinnamon, cashews, date and banana to the quinoa mixture and cook, stirring continuously, for a further 5–10 minutes, or until most of the liquid has been absorbed and the porridge is thick and creamy.

To serve, spoon into bowls and drizzle over the rice malt syrup to finish. Enjoy.

GF | V | VE | DF | EF

nutritional info:
Energy 1485 kj
Calories 355 cal
Protein 8 g
Fibre 13 g
Fat 10 g
Saturated Fat 1 g
Carbs 61 g
Sugar 16 g

Breakfast salad with fried egg

Serves 1 | Preparation time: 5 minutes | Cooking time: 10 minutes

1 tablespoon pine nuts

½ teaspoon olive oil

1 egg

100 g (3½ oz) asparagus, trimmed and diced

2 handfuls of baby spinach leaves

50 g (1¾ oz) cherry tomatoes, quartered

¼ avocado, diced

15 g (½ oz) goat's feta

juice of ½ lemon

sea salt and freshly ground black pepper

Heat a non-stick frying pan over a medium heat, add the pine nuts and toast for 2–3 minutes until lightly golden. Remove from the pan and set aside.

Add the olive oil to the pan and return to the heat, then crack in the egg and fry for 1–2 minutes, or until cooked to your liking. Remove from the pan with a spatula and set aside.

Add the asparagus to the pan and sauté for 3–4 minutes, until softened, then transfer to a bowl together with the spinach, tomatoes, avocado and goat's feta. Squeeze over the lemon juice and season generously with salt and pepper, then toss to combine.

Pile the salad into a serving bowl, top with the fried egg and scatter over the pine nuts. Serve immediately.

nutritional info:
Energy 1301 kj
Calories 311 cal
Protein 15 g
Fibre 7 g
Fat 23 g
Saturated Fat 6 g
Carbs 15 g
Sugar 5 g

GF | V

Healthy gut smoothie

Serves 1 | Preparation time: 5 minutes plus soaking

1 teaspoon chia seeds

1 teaspoon gelatine powder

½ avocado

½ banana

handful of baby spinach leaves

150 g (5½ oz/1 cup) fresh
strawberries, quartered

1 teaspoon ground cinnamon

2 tablespoons vanilla whey
protein powder

2 tablespoons ice cubes

Rich in protein and nutrients, this delicious, naturally sweet smoothie is one of the healthiest breakfast decisions you can make. Though it may sound a little strange, I love to add avocado to my smoothies as it gives them a lovely, creamy texture (not to mention lots of goodness including potassium and the same monounsaturated fatty acids found in olive oil that are thought to be responsible for its beneficial health effects).

Add the chia seeds and gelatine powder to a high-speed blender together with 250 ml (8½ fl oz/1 cup) water and leave to soak for 15 minutes.

Add the avocado, banana, spinach, strawberries and cinnamon to the chia seed mixture and whiz together briefly, then add the protein powder and ice and whiz together until smooth. Pour into a glass or a suitable container to enjoy on the go.

Note: It's optional to fancy these up, as pictured, with nut butter on the rims and, variously, shaved coconut, pepitas, goji berries and cacao nibs. But note the nutritionals won't look quite so good!

nutritional info:
Energy 1280 kj
Calories 306 cal
Protein 13 g
Fibre 14 g
Fat 14 g
Saturated Fat 2 g
Carbs 38 g
Sugar 17 g

GF | EF | NF

Green machine smoothie

Serves 1 | **Preparation time: 5 minutes**

250 ml (8½ fl oz/1 cup) almond milk

1 tablespoon chia seeds

handful of baby spinach leaves

1 teaspoon almond butter

½ avocado

½ frozen banana

1 teaspoon ground cinnamon

Add all of the ingredients to a high–speed blender or food processor and whiz everything together until nice and smooth. Pour into a glass and enjoy.

GF | V | VE | DF | EF

nutritional info:
Energy 1389 kj
Calories 332 cal
Protein 8 g
Fibre 14 g
Fat 20 g
Saturated Fat 2 g
Carbs 31 g
Sugar 14 g

Chocolate for breakfast smoothie

Serves 1 | **Preparation time: 5 minutes plus soaking**

1 tablespoon chia seeds

50 ml (1¾ fl oz) coconut milk

1 banana

1 teaspoon cacao powder

1 teaspoon cacao nibs, plus extra to serve

1 teaspoon maca powder

1 teaspoon ground cinnamon

8 ice cubes

2 tablespoons vanilla whey protein powder

Given this tastes like dessert you might be surprised to find it sitting here on the breakfast menu, but this smoothie makes for the perfect start to a day. Also known as Peruvian ginseng, maca powder is a nutrient-dense wholefood available in good health-food stores that is great for rebalancing our hormones – increasing our focus and energy levels.

Add the chia seeds together with the coconut milk, banana, and 250 ml (8½ fl oz/1 cup) water to a high-speed blender or food processor and leave to soak for 15 minutes.

Once soaked, add the cacao, cacao nibs, maca powder, cinnamon and ice to the blender and whiz together until smooth. Add the protein powder and pulse briefly to combine, then pour into a glass and scatter over a few extra cacao nibs to finish. Enjoy.

nutritional info:
Energy 1519 kj
Calories 363 cal
Protein 14 g
Fibre 27 g
Fat 8 g
Saturated Fat 4 g
Carbs 67 g
Sugar 18 g

GF | V | EF | NF

Lunch.

Boring sandwiches are a thing of the past.
Lunch should be simple, tasty and fulfilling, and we
guarantee these recipes are all that and more.

Creamy vegetable soup

Serves 4 | Preparation time: 5 minutes | Cooking time: 25 minutes

1 tablespoon coconut oil

2 garlic cloves, finely chopped

750 ml (25½ fl oz/3 cups) vegetable stock

½ large cauliflower head, broken into florets and finely chopped

2 zucchini (courgettes), diced

2 carrots, diced

2 teaspoons ground turmeric

1 teaspoon chilli flakes, plus extra if necessary

400 ml (13½ fl oz) coconut cream

sea salt and freshly ground black pepper

4 slices Hidden Veggie Bread (see page 192)

This is such a popular recipe. It not only tastes delicious, but it's packed with vegetables and so easy to make. Serve it with a side of our bread, and you won't even miss the store-bought variety.

Melt the coconut oil in a large saucepan over a medium heat, add the garlic and sauté for 2–3 minutes until golden. Add the stock, vegetables and spices, bring to a simmer and cook, covered, for 20 minutes or until the vegetables are soft.

Remove the pan from the heat and set aside to cool slightly, then transfer the soup to a food processor and blend until smooth.

Pour the soup back into the pan, stir through the coconut cream and return to a simmer. Season to taste. Divide among bowls and serve with slices of hidden veggie bread.

V | GF | DF

nutritional info:
Energy 1277 kj
Calories 438 cal
Protein 14 g
Fibre 11 g
Fat 32 g
Saturated Fat 18 g
Carbs 29 g
Sugar 12 g

Snez's kale & brussels sprout salad with tahini dressing

Serves 1 | Preparation time: 10 minutes

¼ bunch curly or tuscan kale (cavolo nero), stems removed and leaves stripped and finely sliced

pinch of sea salt

pinch of freshly ground black pepper

5 brussels sprouts, shredded

2 tablespoons toasted almonds

TAHINI DRESSING

1 tablespoon tahini

1 tablespoon lemon juice

½ garlic clove, crushed

Snez loves her greens and believes tahini is the key to all good salad dressings. This recipe is so delicious – even kale sceptics should give it a go.

Add the kale leaves to a bowl together with the salt and pepper. Using your hands, gently massage the leaves for 30 seconds or so (this helps soften the kale), then add the brussels sprouts and toss everything together well.

To make the dressing, put all the ingredients in a small bowl and whisk together until well combined.

To serve, pile the salad onto a plate, drizzle over the dressing and scatter over the toasted almonds to finish.

nutritional info:
Energy 1607 kj
Calories 384 cal
Protein 16 g
Fibre 13 g
Fat 29 g
Saturated Fat 3 g
Carbs 8 g
Sugar 7 g

V | VE | EF | DF

Grilled chicken with peach & pistachio salad

Serves 4 | Preparation time: 5 minutes | Cooking time: 7 minutes

2 large peaches, sliced

2 tablespoons rice malt syrup

60 ml (2 fl oz/¼ cup) coconut oil, melted

400 g (14 oz) boneless, skinless chicken breast, cut into strips

150 g (5½ oz) rocket (arugula)

35 g (1¼ oz/¼ cup) pistachio nuts, roughly chopped

30 g (1 oz) goat's feta, crumbled

handful of basil leaves, roughly chopped

sea salt and freshly ground black pepper

DRESSING

2 tablespoons olive oil

60 ml (2 fl oz/¼ cup) apple cider vinegar

1 tablespoon rice malt syrup

juice of 1 lemon

½ teaspoon sea salt

A delicious summery meal ready in minutes. The dressing will last up to two weeks in the fridge.

To make the dressing, simply place all the ingredients in a jar, seal with a lid and shake until well combined.

Add the peach slices to a bowl, pour over the rice malt syrup and toss together gently. Set aside.

Heat the coconut oil on a large chargrill pan or barbecue chargrill to medium–high. Chargrill the chicken pieces for 3–5 minutes on each side, until golden and cooked through. Set aside.

Chargrill the peach slices for 1–2 minutes on each side until golden.

Place the rocket, pistachios, feta and basil leaves in a large serving bowl and toss together well. Add the grilled chicken strips and peach slices and toss again, then drizzle over the dressing. Season to taste and serve.

GF | EF

nutritional info:
Energy 1766 kj
Calories 422 cal
Protein 24 g
Fibre 3 g
Fat 32 g
Saturated Fat 16 g
Carbs 11 g
Sugar 8 g

Prawn salad

Serves 2 | Preparation time: 20 minutes plus marinating | Cooking time: 6 minutes

1 red chilli, finely chopped

1 garlic clove, finely chopped

2 tablespoons olive oil

juice and zest of 1 lemon

250 g (9 oz) peeled raw prawns (shrimp), deveined

½ head iceberg lettuce, roughly chopped

2 celery stalks, diced

125 g (4½ oz) cherry tomatoes, quartered

½ avocado, diced

1 tablespoon finely chopped chives

1 tablespoon sunflower kernels

sea salt and freshly ground black pepper

Put the chilli, garlic, olive oil, lemon zest and half the lemon juice in a mixing bowl, add the prawns and mix everything together well. Cover with plastic wrap and leave to marinate for 20 minutes.

In a large salad bowl, combine the lettuce, celery, tomatoes, avocado, chives and sunflower kernels.

Heat a barbecue grill on high, add the prawns and cook for 2–3 minutes on each side, until golden brown and cooked through. Toss the prawns through the salad and squeeze over the remaining lemon juice. Season well and enjoy.

nutritional info:
Energy 1414 kj
Calories 338 cal
Protein 29 g
Fibre 5 g
Fat 20 g
Saturated Fat 3 g
Carbs 10 g
Sugar 4 g

GF | DF | EF | NF

Miso-baked salmon with broccoli & kale rice

Serves 2 | Preparation time: 10 minutes | Cooking time: 20 minutes

5 teaspoons miso paste

1 tablespoon mirin

2 x 150 g (5½ oz) salmon fillets

lemon wedges, to serve

BROCCOLI & KALE RICE

1 large broccoli head, broken into florets

2 teaspoons olive oil

1 garlic clove, crushed

30 g (1 oz) kale, stems removed and leaves roughly chopped

sea salt and freshly ground black pepper

100 g (3½ oz/⅔ cup) peas, fresh or frozen

1 tablespoon tamari or soy sauce

Miso is a fermented paste made from soybeans commonly used as a Japanese seasoning. I love to use miso for flavour as well as for variety as an alternative to salt or soy sauce. A bonus is that it's packed with B12.

Preheat the oven to 200°C (400°F) and line a baking tray with baking paper.

Place the broccoli florets in a food processor and blitz together briefly into tiny rice-like pieces. Set aside.

Combine the miso paste and mirin in a small bowl. Rub the mixture over the salmon fillets evenly, then place on the prepared baking tray skin-side down and bake for 15 minutes, or until cooked through.

Meanwhile, make the broccoli and kale rice. Heat the oil in a frying pan over a high heat, add the broccoli and garlic and stir-fry for 5 minutes, or until slightly softened. Stir through the kale and cook until it wilts, about 1–2 minutes. Season to taste, then add the peas and tamari and toss to combine.

Spoon the broccoli and kale rice into bowls and top with the salmon fillets. Serve with lemon wedges for squeezing.

nutritional info:
Energy 1226 kj
Calories 293 cal
Protein 40 g
Fibre 5 g
Fat 8 g
Saturated Fat 1 g
Carbs 20 g
Sugar 8 g

GF | NF | EF | DF

Greek lamb salad

Serves 4 | Preparation time: 10 minutes plus marinating | Cooking time: 10 minutes

4 x 100 g (3½ oz) lamb loin fillets

1 cos (romaine) lettuce, leaves separated

200 g (7 oz) cherry tomatoes, quartered

1 cucumber, diced

30 g (1 oz) goat's feta, crumbled

1 tablespoon olive oil

juice of ½ lemon

sea salt and freshly ground black pepper

MARINADE

1 teaspoon chopped oregano

60 ml (2 fl oz/¼ cup) olive oil

1 garlic clove, finely chopped

juice and zest of ½ lemon

This simple lamb salad needs a little advance preparation to get the meat in the marinade, but once that's done it's very quick to pull together. The Greek flavours here are subtle but fresh and perfect for warmer weather.

Combine all the marinade ingredients in a large bowl, add the lamb fillets and toss to coat evenly. Cover with plastic wrap and leave to marinate for 4–6 hours.

Once marinated, heat a chargrill pan or barbecue grill on medium–high, add the lamb fillets and grill for 6 minutes, turning each minute, until browned and cooked through. Remove from the pan and leave to rest for 3–4 minutes before cutting into thick slices.

Meanwhile, add the lettuce leaves, tomatoes, cucumber, feta, olive oil and lemon juice to a large serving bowl and toss together well. Season generously with salt and pepper, add the rested lamb slices and toss again, then serve.

nutritional info:
Energy 1494 kj
Calories 357 cal
Protein 32 g
Fibre 4 g
Fat 26 g
Saturated Fat 7 g
Carbs 11 g
Sugar 5 g

GF | EF | NF

Walnut & basil zucchetti

Serves 2 | Preparation time: 5 minutes | Cooking time: 14 minutes

1 tablespoon olive oil

2 garlic cloves, finely chopped

1 x 400 g (14 oz) tin chopped tomatoes

handful of basil, chopped

½ small red chilli, deseeded and finely chopped (optional)

sea salt and freshly ground black pepper

handful of baby spinach leaves, chopped

2 large button mushrooms, diced

4 tomatoes, quartered

2 tablespoons chopped walnuts

2 small zucchini (courgettes)

1 tablespoon freshly grated parmesan, to serve

Zucchini noodles are popular right now and with good reason, they make a fantastic low-carbohydrate, grain-free alternate to traditional pasta. I like to make this one up in large batches as it keeps really well – leftovers can be stored in the fridge in a suitable container for 2–3 days or frozen for up to 3 months.

Heat the olive oil in a large saucepan over a medium heat, add the garlic and sauté for 2–3 minutes, or until lightly golden.

Add the chopped tomatoes, basil and chilli to the pan and season generously with salt and pepper. Bring to a simmer and cook for 10 minutes, then stir through the spinach, mushrooms and tomatoes. Simmer for a further 2–3 minutes, then stir through the walnuts, remove from the heat and set aside.

Using a spiraliser, cut the zucchini into fine vegetable noodles. (If you do not own a spiraliser, simply shave the zucchini into thin slices with a vegetable peeler or a mandoline.)

Add the zucchetti to the hot sauce and toss to combine. Divide among bowls and scatter over the parmesan to serve.

nutritional info:
**Energy 1293 kj
Calories 308 cal
Protein 12 g
Fibre 10 g
Fat 20 g
Saturated Fat 3 g
Carbs 19 g
Sugar 14 g**

GF | V | EF

Spicy Mexican bowl with avocado

Serves 2 | Preparation time: 5 minutes | Cooking time: 15 minutes

1 teaspoon olive oil

1 garlic clove, crushed

100 g (3½ oz/½ cup) quinoa, rinsed

250 ml (8½ fl oz/1 cup) vegetable stock

100 g (3½ oz) tinned kidney beans, rinsed and drained

50 g (1¾ oz) tinned corn kernels, rinsed and drained

100 g (3½ oz) cherry tomatoes

1 teaspoon ground cumin

1 teaspoon smoked paprika

½ teaspoon chilli flakes

sea salt and freshly ground black pepper

juice of 1 lime

¼ avocado, mashed

2 handfuls of coriander (cilantro) leaves, roughly chopped

I love spicy food, and these bowls packed with vibrant Mexican flavours are no exception. Chilli flakes are a great metabolism booster, so feel free to add more to your liking here (well, that's my excuse ...).

Heat the olive oil in a large saucepan over a medium–high heat. Add the garlic and sauté for 30 seconds until fragrant, then add the quinoa, vegetable stock, kidney beans, corn, tomatoes and spices. Season to taste and bring to the boil, then reduce to a simmer and cook, covered, for 12 minutes or until the quinoa is tender and all the liquid has been absorbed.

Remove from the heat and stir through the lime juice. Spoon into bowls, top with the avocado and scatter over the chopped coriander to serve.

GF | DF | V | VE | EF | NF

nutritional info:
Energy 1305 kj
Calories 312 cal
Protein 11 g
Fibre 9 g
Fat 9 g
Saturated Fat 1 g
Carbs 51 g
Sugar 5 g

Sweet potato & zucchini fritters with smoked salmon & avocado

Serves 4 | Preparation time: 5 minutes | Cooking time: 10 minutes

1 zucchini (courgette), grated

1 small sweet potato, grated

2 handfuls of coriander (cilantro) leaves, roughly chopped

2 eggs, beaten

2 teaspoons ground cumin

2 tablespoons psyllium husks

35 g (1¼ oz/¼ cup) coconut flour, sifted

1 tablespoon coconut oil

TO SERVE

100 g (3½ oz) smoked salmon

2 avocados, mashed

freshly ground black pepper

1 lemon, cut into wedges

Who doesn't love fritters? These are one of my favourites. Sweet potato is an excellent natural carbohydrate, rich in fibre and when combined with protein and good fats from eggs and avocado, it's great for blood sugar control.

Mix together the zucchini, sweet potato, coriander and beaten eggs in a large bowl, then add the cumin, psyllium husks and coconut flour and mix together really well to form a nice, thick batter.

Divide the fritter mixture evenly into eight pieces and use your hands to shape each into balls.

Melt the coconut oil in a large frying pan over a medium heat. Add the fritters and flatten slightly with the back of a spoon, then cook for 3–4 minutes on each side until cooked through and golden and crispy on the outside.

To serve, divide the fritters among plates and top with the smoked salmon and mashed avocado. Season with freshly ground black pepper and serve with lemon wedges for squeezing.

nutritional info:
Energy 1293 kj
Calories 309 cal
Protein 12 g
Fibre 14 g
Fat 18 g
Saturated Fat 5 g
Carbs 26 g
Sugar 3 g

GF | DF | NF

Spring vegetable quiche

Serves 6 | Preparation time: 10 minutes | Cooking time: 20 minutes

BASE

170 g (6 oz/1½ cups) almond flour

65 g (2¼ oz/½ cup) coconut flour

1 teaspoon gluten-free baking powder

½ teaspoon sea salt

2 eggs, beaten

60 ml (2 fl oz/¼ cup) coconut oil, melted

FILLING

5 eggs

handful of button or enoki mushrooms, finely chopped

½ leek, finely sliced

200 g (7 oz) asparagus, trimmed and finely sliced

80 g (2¾ oz/½ cup) peas, fresh or frozen

sea salt and freshly ground black pepper

GF | V | DF

We use a combination of almond and coconut flour in this quiche as an alternative to standard flour and to change the nutrient balance. Increasing the protein and good fats and decreasing carbohydrates will keep you fuller for longer and keep cravings at bay.

Preheat the oven to 180°C (350°F). Lightly grease a 28 cm (11 in) quiche dish with a little coconut oil.

For the base, combine the flours, baking powder and salt in a large mixing bowl, then stir in the beaten egg and melted coconut oil to form a dough.

Using your hands, carefully press the pastry lightly into the base and sides of the greased dish, being careful to spread it evenly. Bake for 10 minutes or until lightly golden. Remove from the oven and set aside to cool slightly.

To make the filling, beat the eggs in a bowl and stir in the mushrooms, leek, asparagus and peas. Season with salt and pepper.

Pour the filling over the cooked base, return to the oven and bake for another 10 minutes, or until set and firm to the touch. Remove from the oven and leave to cool before slicing and serving.

nutritional info:
Energy 1506 kj
Calories 360 cal
Protein 14 g
Fibre 8 g
Fat 29 g
Saturated Fat 12 g
Carbs 15 g
Sugar 3 g

Mushroom burger

Serves 2 | Preparation time: 5 minutes | Cooking time: 10 minutes

4 portobello mushrooms

75 g (2¾ oz) goat's cheese, crumbled

1 teaspoon dried or fresh thyme

2 bacon rashers

2 eggs

½ tomato, sliced

½ avocado, mashed

1 beetroot, grated

½ carrot, grated

handful of rocket (arugula)

sea salt and freshly ground black pepper

While everyone loves a burger, a stodgy bun can make it a bit of a blowout meal. That's why I love these burgers, which use portobello mushrooms as a delicious, low-carbohydrate and grain-free alternative for sandwiching all those brilliant fillings together. You won't miss the bun, I promise.

Preheat the oven to 180°C (350°F) and line a baking tray with baking paper.

Arrange the mushrooms stalk up on the prepared baking tray. Bake for 4 minutes, then top with the goat's cheese and thyme and bake for a further 3 minutes, or until the mushrooms are tender and the goat's cheese has started to melt.

Meanwhile heat a chargrill pan over a medium heat, add the bacon and cook for 3–4 minutes until crispy. Remove from the pan and set aside to drain on paper towel.

Crack an egg into the pan and fry in the bacon juices for 1–2 minutes or until cooked to your liking. Remove from the pan with a spatula and set aside, then repeat with the remaining egg.

To serve, place one of the mushrooms on a plate and top with a bacon rasher, a fried egg and half of the tomato, mashed avocado, beetroot, carrot and rocket. Season generously with salt and pepper and top with another mushroom to sandwich the burger together, then repeat with the remaining mushrooms and fillings.

nutritional info:
Energy 1962 kj
Calories 469 cal
Protein 27 g
Fibre 9 g
Fat 34 g
Saturated Fat 14 g
Carbs 11 g
Sugar 6 g

GF | NF

Pumpkin curry with brown rice

Serves 4 | Preparation time: 10 minutes | Cooking time: 55 minutes

200 g (7 oz/1 cup) brown rice

30 g (1 oz/¼ cup) pepitas (pumpkin seeds)

1 kg (2 lb 3 oz) pumpkin (winter squash), peeled and cut into 2 cm (¾ in) cubes

1 large eggplant (aubergine), cut into 2 cm (¾ in) cubes

2 tablespoons miso paste

2 tablespoons red curry paste

1 tablespoon coconut oil

2 tablespoons lemon juice

400 g (14 oz) snow peas (mangetout), roughly chopped

1 teaspoon olive oil

sea salt and freshly ground black pepper

½ red onion, finely sliced

150 g (5½ oz/3 cups) baby spinach leaves

½ bunch of mint, roughly chopped

Not like a traditional pumpkin curry but a great vegetarian meal for Meat Free Monday. This is one Snez and I often cook in double batches on a Sunday, to ensure we have food prepped for a busy week ahead.

Preheat the oven to 200°C (400°F) and line a baking tray with baking paper.

Add the rice to a saucepan, cover with 170 ml (5½ fl oz/⅔ cup) water and bring to a boil. Cover with a lid, reduce the heat to a simmer and cook for 25 minutes. Drain off any remaining water and rinse the rice under cool water, then set aside until needed.

Meanwhile, spread the pepitas on the prepared baking tray in an even layer and bake for 5–10 minutes, or until lightly golden. Remove from the baking tray and set aside.

Add the pumpkin and eggplant to the baking tray together with the miso paste, curry paste, coconut oil and half the lemon juice and mix together well to coat evenly. Bake for 30 minutes until lightly golden and soft. Leave to cool slightly, then transfer to a large bowl.

Add the snow peas to a steamer set over simmering water and steam for 2–3 minutes, or until just tender. Refresh under cold water, then add to the bowl with the pumpkin and eggplant.

Whisk the olive oil and remaining lemon juice together in a small bowl and season to taste. Pour over the cooked veg and toss to combine, then add the onion, spinach, rice and mint and toss together again. Divide among plates, scatter over the toasted pepitas and serve.

nutritional info:
Energy 1592 kj
Calories 379 cal
Protein 17 g
Fibre 11 g
Fat 13 g
Saturated Fat 5 g
Carbs 58 g
Sugar 12 g

GF | V | VE | NF | EF | DF

Quinoa salad with poached chicken

Serves 2 | Preparation time: 10 minutes | Cooking time: 20 minutes

200 g (7 oz) boneless, skinless chicken breast, cut into thin strips

500 ml (17 fl oz/2 cups) vegetable stock

1 tablespoon pine nuts

1½ teaspoons olive oil

½ red onion finely chopped

1 garlic clove, crushed

1 teaspoon dried thyme

50 g (1¾ oz/¼ cup) quinoa, rinsed

handful of kale, stems removed and leaves finely chopped

40 g (1½ oz/¼ cup) sun-dried tomatoes, roughly chopped

30 g (1 oz) feta, crumbled

Chicken is such a simple protein to use – it's quick to cook, nutrient dense and versatile. I love to poach chicken with vegetable stock for more flavour and to keep the breast from drying out.

Place the chicken and stock in a medium saucepan over a low–medium heat. Bring to a very gentle simmer, cover with a lid and poach for 10 minutes, then remove the pan from the heat and leave to stand for 5 minutes. Remove the chicken from the hot stock using a slotted spoon and set aside.

Meanwhile, heat a frying pan over a medium heat, add the pine nuts and toast for 2–3 minutes until lightly golden. Remove from the pan and set aside.

Add the oil, onion, garlic and thyme to the frying pan and cook for 2–3 minutes, or until the onion has started to soften. Add the quinoa and 125 ml (4 fl oz/½ cup) water and bring to a simmer, then cover with a lid and cook for 10 minutes. Add the kale and sun-dried tomatoes and cook, covered, for another 2–3 minutes, until the kale has softened and all the liquid has been absorbed.

Add the pine nuts and feta to the pan with the quinoa and mix everything together well. Season to taste, then divide among plates and top with the poached chicken pieces. Serve.

nutritional info:
Energy 1398 kj
Calories 330 cal
Protein 27 g
Fibre 2 g
Fat 16 g
Saturated Fat 2 g
Carbs 22 g
Sugar 4 g

GF | EF

Tofu san choy bao

Serves 2 | Preparation time: 5 minutes | Cooking time: 15 minutes

1 teaspoon coconut oil

250 g (9 oz) firm tofu, diced

150 g (5½ oz) mushrooms, finely diced

50 g (1¾ oz) kale, stems removed and leaves finely chopped

1 red chilli, finely chopped

1 tablespoon grated fresh ginger

1 garlic clove, crushed

4 spring onions (scallions), finely sliced

1 tablespoon sesame oil

60 ml (2 fl oz/¼ cup) tamari or soy sauce

sea salt and freshly ground black pepper

4 large iceberg lettuce leaves

handful of roughly chopped coriander (cilantro) leaves, to serve

Tofu, also known as bean curd, is an excellent vegetarian source of protein. Rich in iron and calcium, it's great as an alternative to meat and seafood. It soaks up flavours from sauces, soups and spices and is put to good work here in our tofu san choy bao.

Melt the coconut oil in a frying pan over a high heat. Add the tofu, mushrooms, kale, chilli, ginger, garlic, spring onions, sesame oil and tamari and sauté for 15 minutes, or until the mushrooms are tender and the tofu is nicely browned. Season to taste, remove from the heat and leave to cool slightly.

Arrange the lettuce leaves on a serving plate. To serve, spoon a generous helping of the tofu mixture into each of your lettuce 'cups' and scatter over a little chopped coriander, then wrap up and enjoy.

GF | V | VE | DF | EF | NF

nutritional info:
Energy 1611 kj
Calories 385 cal
Protein 25 g
Fibre 7 g
Fat 30 g
Saturated Fat 5 g
Carbs 38 g
Sugar 14 g

Beetroot, goat's cheese & walnut salad

Serves 4 | Preparation time: 5 minutes | Cooking time: 45 minutes

4 large beetroot

60 ml (2 fl oz/¼ cup) coconut oil, melted

50 g (1¾ oz/½ cup) walnut halves

2 tablespoons rice malt syrup

200 g (7 oz) rocket (arugula)

50 g (1¾ oz) soft goat's cheese, crumbled

DRESSING

60 ml (2 fl oz/¼ cup) extra-virgin olive oil

1 tablespoon apple cider vinegar

½ teaspoon sea salt

Beetroot, goat's cheese and walnuts are such a winning combination in a salad. Leftovers are great topped with a tin of tuna or salmon for lunch the next day.

Preheat the oven to 180°C (350°F).

Prick the beetroot all over with a fork, rub with the coconut oil and arrange on a baking tray. Bake for 45 minutes, or until tender. Set aside to cool, then peel and cut into 2 cm (¾ in) cubes.

Heat a frying pan over a low heat, add the walnuts and rice malt syrup and stir together to coat evenly. Cook, stirring, for 2–3 minutes, or until lightly browned all over, then remove from the heat and set aside to cool.

In a small bowl, whisk together the dressing ingredients until well combined.

Add the rocket and beetroot to a large serving bowl and toss together well. Top with the goat's cheese and walnuts, then drizzle over the dressing. Serve.

nutritional info:
Energy 1833 kj
Calories 438 cal
Protein 7 g
Fibre 4 g
Fat 41 g
Saturated Fat 17 g
Carbs 16 g
Sugar 10 g

GF | V | EF

Pork tenderloin & cauliflower salad

Serves 4 | Preparation time: 10 minutes | Cooking time: 40 minutes

60 ml (2 fl oz/¼ cup) coconut oil, melted

1 tablespoon ground cumin

1 tablespoon paprika

1 teaspoon garlic powder

1 teaspoon sea salt

1 small cauliflower head, broken into florets

1 fennel bulb, cut into thin wedges

4 x 100 g (3½ oz) pork tenderloins

1 teaspoon olive oil

50 g (1¾ oz) baby spinach leaves

2 tablespoons pepitas (pumpkin seeds)

sea salt and freshly ground black pepper

Cauliflower is such a versatile vegetable, as well as being nutrient-rich and an effective way to lower the carbohydrate content of a meal. Cauliflower salad is a great support act to other proteins too.

Preheat the oven to 180°C (350°F).

Add the coconut oil, cumin, paprika, garlic powder and salt to a large mixing bowl and mix together well. Add the cauliflower and fennel and toss together to coat evenly in the spices, then transfer to a baking tray and arrange in an even layer. Roast for 40 minutes, turning halfway through cooking, until the vegetables are golden brown and tender.

Ten minutes before the vegetables are done, brush the pork with the olive oil and heat a chargrill pan or barbecue grill on medium–high.

Add the pork to the hot pan and grill for 6 minutes, turning each minute, until browned and cooked through. Remove from the pan and leave to rest for 3–4 minutes before cutting into thick slices.

Add the rested pork slices to a large serving bowl together with the spinach and pepitas and toss to combine. Add the roasted cauliflower and fennel, toss again and season generously to taste. Serve.

nutritional info:
Energy 1485 kj
Calories 355 cal
Protein 28 g
Fibre 9 g
Fat 21 g
Saturated Fat 14 g
Carbs 19 g
Sugar 8 g

GF | DF | EF | NF

Vietnamese prawn rolls with ginger tamari dipping sauce

Serves 1 (makes 4) | Preparation time: 15 minutes

4 iceberg lettuce leaves

100 g (3½ oz) peeled raw prawns (shrimp), cut in half lengthways

¼ red capsicum (bell pepper), seeds removed and cut into matchsticks

1 celery stalk, cut into matchsticks

4 snow peas (mangetout), finely sliced lengthways

1 carrot, cut into matchsticks

1 Lebanese (short) cucumber, cut into matchsticks

¼ bunch mint, leaves picked

¼ bunch basil, leaves picked

DIPPING SAUCE

1½ teaspoons tamari or soy sauce

1 tablespoon olive oil

1 teaspoon sesame seeds

1 tablespoon grated fresh ginger

GF | DF | EF | NF

Stuffed full of a rainbow-like selection of veggies and lovely, juicy prawns, these Vietnamese rolls deliver big on the flavour front while also being a source of protein and nutrients. For a veggie version of these rolls, switch out the prawns for 100 g (3½ oz) of firm tofu, grilled and cut into strips.

To make the dipping sauce, place all the ingredients in a bowl and mix well to combine.

Lay the lettuce leaves out flat and divide the prawns, vegetables and herbs between the leaves. Carefully roll the lettuce leaves up and eat immediately with the dipping sauce or secure with a toothpick and transfer to a serving plate for enjoying later.

nutritional info:
Energy 1422 kj
Calories 340 cal
Protein 30 g
Fibre 7 g
Fat 19 g
Saturated Fat 3 g
Carbs 9 g
Sugar 8 g

Raw pad Thai salad with poached chicken

Serves 1 | Preparation time: 15 minutes | Cooking time: 10 minutes

150 g (5½ oz) chicken tenderloins

1 small zucchini (courgette)

1 carrot

¼ red capsicum (bell pepper)

45 g (1½ oz) Chinese cabbage (wombok)

6 snow peas (mangetout)

1 teaspoon sesame seeds

¼ bunch of basil, leaves picked

¼ bunch of mint, leaves picked

DRESSING

1 garlic clove, crushed

1½ teaspoons crunchy peanut butter

1 tablespoon lime juice

½ teaspoon honey

This salad is full of crunchy textures and bright flavours, perfect for a hot summer's day. To make it vegetarian, replace the poached chicken with 100 g (3½ oz) of sautéed cubed firm tofu.

Bring a small saucepan of water to the boil over a high heat. Carefully lower the chicken pieces into the water, then turn off the heat and cover with a lid. Leave for 10 minutes to poach, then remove the chicken with a slotted spoon and set aside.

Using a spiraliser or mandoline, cut the vegetables into very fine slices. Transfer to a large bowl.

Heat a small saucepan over a medium heat, add the sesame seeds and toast for 2–3 minutes, stirring, until lightly golden. Remove from the pan and set aside.

For the dressing, add the ingredients to the same pan, reduce the heat to low and cook, stirring, until everything is well combined and nicely warm (you may need to add a tablespoon or so of hot water to thin the dressing if it's looking a little thick).

Pour the warm dressing over the sliced vegetables, add the chicken pieces and toss together to coat well. To serve, pile the salad onto a plate and scatter over the herbs and toasted sesame seeds.

nutritional info:
Energy 1405 kj
Calories 335 cal
Protein 41 g
Fibre 8 g
Fat 11 g
Saturated Fat 2 g
Carbs 13 g
Sugar 12 g

GF | EF | DF

Broccoli fried rice with prawns

Serves 4 | Preparation time: 10 minutes | Cooking time: 15 minutes

1 broccoli head, broken into florets

1½ tablespoons coconut oil

4 eggs, lightly beaten

1 red chilli, diced

3 bacon rashers, diced

1 red capsicum (bell pepper), diced

1 carrot, diced

¼ cauliflower head, broken into florets and roughly chopped

3 celery stalks, diced

80 g (2¾ oz/½ cup) peas, fresh or frozen

2 tablespoons tamari or soy sauce

1 tablespoon fish sauce

sea salt and freshly ground black pepper

300 g (10½ oz) peeled raw prawns (shrimp), deveined

1 bunch coriander (cilantro) leaves, roughly chopped

GF | DF | NF

I love to whip up this lunch on the weekend when I have a bit more time, making up extra so that I have leftovers for the week. Prawns are a great source of protein that really complement the Asian flavours here.

Place the broccoli florets in a food processor and blitz together briefly into tiny rice-like pieces. Set aside.

Melt ½ tablespoon of coconut oil in a large frying pan or a wok over a medium heat. Add the eggs and swirl over the base to form an omelette, then cook for 2 minutes or until set. Transfer to a chopping board and set aside to cool slightly, then cut into short strips.

Add ½ tablespoon of the remaining oil to the hot pan together with the chilli and bacon and stir-fry over a medium–high heat for 2–3 minutes, or until browned. Add the capsicum, carrot, cauliflower, celery and peas to the pan and stir-fry for a further 2–3 minutes until tender, then add the broccoli 'rice' and sauté for 2–3 minutes, until slightly softened. Stir in the tamari and fish sauce, toss through the egg strips and season with salt and pepper, then remove from the heat and spoon into serving bowls.

Heat the remaining coconut oil in a frying pan over a high heat, add the prawns and cook for 3 minutes on each side until golden. Divide between the serving bowls, scatter over the chopped coriander and enjoy.

nutritional info:
Energy 1226 kj
Calories 293 cal
Protein 28 g
Fibre 5 g
Fat 14 g
Saturated Fat 6 g
Carbs 13 g
Sugar 3 g

Tuna & quinoa salad with olives

Serves 2 | Preparation time: 5 minutes | Cooking time: 15 minutes

50 g (1¾ oz/¼ cup) quinoa, rinsed

250 g (9 oz) tinned tuna, drained

1 red chilli, finely diced

1 garlic clove, crushed

1 tablespoon olive oil

200 g (7 oz) broccolini, roughly sliced

55 g (2 oz/⅓ cup) green olives, sliced

2 tomatoes, diced

100 g (3½ oz) rocket (arugula)

1 tablespoon chopped parsley

sea salt and freshly ground black pepper

Bring 125 ml (4 fl oz/½ cup) water to the boil in a saucepan, add the quinoa, cover with a lid and cook for 15 minutes, fluffing up the grains halfway through cooking with a fork for extra volume, until the grains are tender and the water has been absorbed. Set aside to cool.

In a small bowl, toss the drained tuna together with the chilli, garlic and olive oil.

Add the broccolini to a steamer set over simmering water and steam for 4–5 minutes, or until just tender. Set aside.

In a large serving bowl combine cooked quinoa with the tuna, broccolini, olives, tomatoes, rocket and parsley. Toss well to combine and season generously with salt and pepper. Serve.

nutritional info:
Energy 1920 kj
Calories 459 cal
Protein 36 g
Fibre 6 g
Fat 16 g
Saturated Fat 2 g
Carbs 40 g
Sugar 4 g

GF | DF | EF | NF

Warm chicken salad

Serves 1 | Preparation time: 5 minutes | Cooking time: 30 minutes

100 g (3½ oz) heirloom carrots, trimmed

¼ teaspoon ground cumin

1½ teaspoons coconut oil, melted

sea salt and freshly ground black pepper

1 bacon rasher, roughly chopped

100 g (3½ oz) boneless, skinless chicken thighs, thinly sliced

¼ avocado, diced

handful of rocket (arugula)

handful of baby spinach leaves

70 g (2½ oz) cherry tomatoes, diced

½ red capsicum (bell pepper), seeds removed and diced

1 tablespoon roughly chopped parsley

juice of ½ lemon

We've chosen to use chicken thighs in this salad as they're generally tastier and, when free range, rich in healthy fats. To save on free-range meat, I like to buy in bulk as chicken freezes so well.

Preheat the oven to 180°C (350°F).

Add the carrots to an ovenproof dish with the cumin and coconut oil. Season with salt and pepper and mix everything together well, then roast for 20 minutes, or until the carrots are lightly golden and tender. Remove from the oven and set aside.

In a frying pan, cook the bacon over a medium heat for 5–6 minutes until golden, then remove from the pan with a slotted spoon and set aside on paper towel to drain. Add the chicken pieces to the pan and cook for 2–3 minutes on each side until nicely golden and cooked through. Set aside.

Add the avocado, rocket, spinach, cherry tomatoes, capsicum and parsley to a serving bowl and toss gently to combine. Add the carrots, bacon and chicken pieces, squeeze over the lemon juice and toss together again. Season to taste and serve.

GF | NF | DF | EF

nutritional info:
Energy 1527 kj
Calories 365 cal
Protein 21 g
Fibre 6 g
Fat 26 g
Saturated Fat 11 g
Carbs 13 g
Sugar 5 g

Broccoli & kale salad

Serves 2 | Preparation time: 5 minutes | Cooking time: 7 minutes

2 broccoli heads, broken into florets and stems cut into 2 cm (¾ in) chunks

2 teaspoons coconut oil

150 g (5½ oz) kale, stems removed and leaves torn

1 tablespoon flaked almonds

3 tablespoons goji berries

½ large avocado, sliced

30 g (1 oz) goat's feta

DRESSING

2 teaspoons olive oil

juice of ½ lemon

pinch of sea salt

While this green veg salad is perfect just as it is, it also makes a lovely side to a nice piece of lean protein such as grilled fish. Try making up extra, then taking the leftovers to work and topping them with a tin of tuna or salmon for some additional omega 3 goodness.

Add the broccoli florets and stem pieces to a steamer set over simmering water and steam for 5 minutes, or until tender. Transfer to a serving bowl and set aside to cool.

Melt the coconut oil in a frying pan over a medium heat, add the kale and sauté for 3 minutes until soft. Add to the bowl with the steamed broccoli pieces and leave to cool.

In a separate bowl, whisk together all the dressing ingredients until well combined.

Add the almonds, goji berries and avocado to the bowl with the cooled vegetables, then pour over the dressing and toss to combine.

To serve, divide the salad between plates and crumble over the feta to finish.

nutritional info:
Energy 1487 kj
Calories 355 cal
Protein 16 g
Fibre 14 g
Fat 24 g
Saturated Fat 8 g
Carbs 11 g
Sugar 11 g

V | GF | EF

Summer salad bowl with grilled chicken

Serves 4 | Preparation time: 5 minutes | Cooking time: 20 minutes

120 g (4½ oz) pumpkin (winter squash), cut into cubes

½ tablespoon olive oil

¼ teaspoon ground cinnamon

sea salt and freshly ground black pepper

1 zucchini (courgette)

1 carrot

1 baby beetroot

1 corn cob, quartered

600 g (1 lb 5 oz) chicken tenderloins

1 cos (romaine) lettuce, leaves roughly torn

1 red capsicum (bell pepper), sliced

125 g (4½ oz) cherry tomatoes, quartered

2 tablespoons pepitas (pumpkin seeds)

1 avocado, smashed

More chicken, yes. This is one of my favourites because it's simple to make but a great way to impress your guests, showing them how amazing salads can be with the right ingredients. I mean, who doesn't love smashed avocado?

Preheat the oven to 180°C (350°F).

Add the pumpkin, olive oil and cinnamon to a baking tray, season with salt and pepper and mix together well. Roast in the oven for 20 minutes, or until soft and lightly golden.

Using a spiraliser, mandoline or sharp vegetable peeler, cut the zucchini, carrot and beetroot into fine noodles or slices. Transfer to a large serving bowl and set aside.

Add the corn cob pieces to a steamer set over simmering water and steam for 5-6 minutes, or until just tender. Remove from the steamer and set aside to cool, then slice off the kernels and transfer to the bowl with the sliced vegetables.

Heat a barbecue grill on high, add the chicken and cook for 2 minutes, until cooked through and golden brown on all sides.

To serve, add the cos lettuce, capsicum, tomatoes and pepitas to the bowl with the vegetables and toss to combine. Top with the grilled chicken pieces and dollops of smashed avocado and season well. Enjoy.

nutritional info:
Energy 1247 kj
Calories 298 cal
Protein 34 g
Fibre 6 g
Fat 12 g
Saturated Fat 2 g
Carbs 22 g
Sugar 7 g

GF | DF | EF | NF

Dinner.

Your tastebuds will love you and so will your family and friends when you whip up these delicious dinners. You'll never want, or need, to eat takeaway again!

Alex's pan-fried salmon with sweet corn & avocado salsa

Serves 2 | Preparation time: 5 minutes | Cooking time: 10 minutes

2 teaspoons olive oil

2 x 120 g (4½ oz) salmon fillets, skin on

sea salt and freshly ground black pepper

lemon wedges, to serve

SWEET CORN & AVOCADO SALSA

125 g (4½ oz) tinned corn kernels, rinsed and drained

250 g (9 oz) cherry tomatoes, halved

½ avocado, diced

¼ red onion, diced

2 handfuls of coriander (cilantro) leaves, chopped

2 teaspoons olive oil

1 teaspoon red wine vinegar

pinch of sea salt

pinch of freshly ground black pepper

GF | NF | EF | DF

Alex is my younger brother and he's great in the kitchen. This meal is a 28 favourite and the sweet corn and avocado salsa gives it a Mexican twist.

For the sweet corn and avocado salsa, add all the ingredients to a bowl and toss together gently to combine. Set aside.

Rub the olive oil over the salmon fillets to coat evenly and season generously with salt and pepper on all sides.

Heat a frying pan over a medium–high heat, add the salmon fillets skin-side down and cook for 2–4 minutes then turn and cook for a further 2–3 minutes, or until the salmon is cooked and breaks into nice flakes when pressed with a fork but still remains a little pink in the centre.

Divide the salsa between serving plates and top with the salmon fillets. Serve with lemon wedges for squeezing.

nutritional info:
Energy 1888 kj
Calories 450 cal
Protein 28 g
Fibre 4 g
Fat 33 g
Saturated Fat 6 g
Carbs 9 g
Sugar 4 g

Eye fillet steak with roasted sweet potato salad

Serves 4 | Preparation time: 5 minutes | Cooking time: 20 minutes

4 x 125 g (4½ oz) eye-fillet steaks

sea salt

ROASTED SWEET POTATO SALAD

2 large sweet potatoes, cut into 1 cm (½ in) cubes

2 tablespoons olive oil

sea salt and freshly ground black pepper

3 eggs

4 bacon rashers, diced

2 spring onions (scallions), finely chopped

6 semi-dried (sun-blushed) tomatoes, finely chopped

handful of rocket (arugula)

1 tablespoon finely chopped chives

4 tablespoons Clean Mayonnaise (see page 160)

nutritional info:
Energy 1837 kj
Calories 439 cal
Protein 36 g
Fibre 2 g
Fat 27 g
Saturated Fat 7 g
Carbs 18 g
Sugar 6 g

Our sweet potato salad is so nourishing and packed with nutrients that you really will only need a palm-sized piece of steak to complement it. Gone are the days of protein being the centrepiece of meal – vegetables run the show here at 28.

Preheat the oven to 180°C (350°F) and line a baking tray with baking paper.

For the roasted sweet potato salad, add the sweet potato and three-quarters of the olive oil to a large bowl and toss together well. Season well with salt and pepper, then transfer to the lined baking tray and roast for 20 minutes or until soft and golden. Remove from the oven and set aside to cool.

Place the eggs in a large saucepan and cover with cold water. Bring to the boil, then reduce the heat to medium and simmer gently for 10 minutes. Remove from the pan and leave to cool under running water, then peel and roughly chop. Set aside.

Meanwhile, dry-fry the bacon in a non-stick frying pan set over a medium heat for 5–6 minutes until golden and crispy. Remove from the pan with a spatula and set aside on paper towel to drain.

In a large serving bowl, combine the roast sweet potato, eggs, bacon, spring onion, semi-dried tomatoes, rocket and chives. Spoon over the mayonnaise and toss together well to ensure everything is evenly coated. Season generously with salt and pepper.

Heat a barbecue chargrill or chargrill pan to high. Season the steaks with salt, transfer to the hot grill and cook for 4 minutes on each side. Remove from the heat and leave to rest for 3–4 minutes, then serve with the roasted sweet potato salad.

GF | DF | NF

Chicken satay stir-fry with cauliflower rice

Serves 4 | Preparation time: 5 minutes | Cooking time: 10 minutes

1 tablespoon coconut oil

500 g (1 lb 2 oz) boneless, skinless chicken thighs, diced

1 red capsicum (bell pepper)

1 carrot

½ broccoli head

60 g (2 oz) green beans, trimmed

60 ml (2 fl oz/¼ cup) chicken stock or chicken bone broth

1 large handful of coriander (cilantro) leaves, roughly chopped

1 x Cauliflower Rice (see page 148), to serve

SATAY SAUCE

65 g (2¼ oz/¼ cup) almond butter

1 teaspoon coconut aminos

1 chopped garlic clove

1 tablespoon grated fresh ginger

3 tablespoons coconut cream

½ teaspoon chilli flakes

juice of 1 lime

1 teaspoon raw honey (optional)

sea salt

GF | DF | EF

This stir-fry is packed full of the flavours of your favourite takeaway with none of the nasties. Leftover satay sauce can be stored in an airtight container in the fridge for up to 5 days – it's the perfect marinade for barbecue chicken or lamb skewers.

To make the satay sauce, put all ingredients in a food processor or high-speed blender and blend until smooth. Set aside.

To prepare the vegetables, cut the capsicum and carrot into strips and break the broccoli into small florets.

Melt the coconut oil in a wok over a high heat. Add the chicken pieces and stir-fry for 2–3 minutes until browned on all sides. Remove from the wok and set aside.

Add the capsicum, carrot, broccoli and green beans to the hot wok and stir-fry for 1 minute, then pour over the chicken stock, bring to a simmer and cook for 5 minutes, or until the vegetables are tender and the liquid has reduced by half. Season to taste.

Return the chicken to the pan together with 3–4 tablespoons of the satay sauce and stir together well, then divide among plates and scatter over the chopped coriander. Serve with the cauliflower rice.

nutritional info:
Energy 1594 kj
Calories 381 cal
Protein 30 g
Fibre 9 g
Fat 20 g
Saturated Fat 5 g
Carbs 33 g
Sugar 11 g

Spicy beef burger salad

Serves 1 | Preparation time: 10 minutes | Cooking time: 10 minutes

100 g (3½ oz) minced (ground) beef

2 eggs, 1 beaten

½ teaspoon garlic powder

½ teaspoon chilli flakes

sea salt and freshly ground black pepper

2 tomatoes, roughly chopped

1 yellow capsicum (bell pepper), seeds removed and roughly chopped

¼ avocado, roughly chopped

handful of coriander (cilantro) leaves, finely chopped

1½ teaspoons olive oil

juice of 1 lime

1 teaspoon coconut oil

2 large iceberg lettuce leaves, shredded

Deconstructed burger salads such as this one are a great way to enjoy your all-time favourite feeds without the added carbohydrates delivered by those buns. Use grass-fed meat and free-range eggs here to make sure you're taking on board as many of those lovely heart-healthy omega-3 fatty acids as possible.

Add the minced beef, beaten egg, garlic powder and chilli flakes to a bowl and mix together well. Season with salt and pepper and shape into a patty using your hands, then set aside.

Place the tomatoes, capsicum and avocado in a serving bowl and toss to combine. Add the coriander, olive oil and lime juice and toss again. Set aside.

Melt the coconut oil in a frying pan over a medium heat, add the beef patty and cook for 3 minutes on each side until browned. Remove from the pan and transfer to paper towel to drain. Add the egg to the pan and fry for 1–2 minutes or until cooked to your liking. Set aside.

Add the lettuce leaves to the bowl with the dressed veg and toss together, then top with the patty and egg. Serve immediately.

nutritional info:
Energy 1702 kj
Calories 407 cal
Protein 23 g
Fibre 5 g
Fat 32 g
Saturated Fat 11 g
Carbs 9 g
Sugar 3 g

GF | DF | NF

Eggplant parma

Serves 2 | Preparation time: 10 minutes | Cooking time: 30 minutes

1 tablespoon olive oil

1 eggplant (aubergine), cut lengthways into 2 cm (¾ in) slices

1 garlic clove, crushed

½ red onion, diced

1 capsicum (bell pepper), seeds removed and diced

75 g (2¾ oz) firm tofu, finely diced

200 g (7 oz) tinned crushed tomatoes

handful of basil leaves, chopped

4 tablespoons tomato paste (concentrated purée)

30 g (1 oz) cheddar cheese, grated

1 tablespoon pine nuts

¼ avocado, sliced

sea salt and freshly ground black pepper

This delicious vegetarian alternative to a traditional parmigiana is gluten-free, grain-free and low in carbohydrates. What's not to love?

Preheat the oven to 180°C (350°F) and grease a medium ramekin with 1 teaspoon of olive oil.

Arrange the eggplant slices in a single layer over a large baking tray and brush with ½ teaspoon of olive oil. Bake for 20 minutes, or until the eggplant is soft, then remove from the oven and leave on the tray to cool.

Heat 1½ teaspoons of the olive oil in a frying pan over a medium–high heat, add the garlic and onion and sauté for 2 minutes, until fragrant. Add the capsicum and tofu and cook for 5 minutes, stirring, or until the capsicum has softened slightly and the tofu is golden brown. Pour over the crushed tomatoes, stir in the basil and bring to a simmer. Cook, stirring, for a further 5 minutes, until slightly thickened and reduced, then remove from the heat and set aside to cool slightly.

Working as if you were constructing a lasagne, add the eggplant slices and spoonfuls of the tomato and tofu mixture to the greased ramekin in alternate layers, spreading the tomato paste over the eggplant slices as you go, until everything has been used up. Top with the cheese and pine nuts and bake in the oven for 10 minutes or until the cheese has melted and the parma is lightly golden.

Remove from the oven and top with the avocado slices. Season to taste and serve.

nutritional info:
Energy 1606 kj
Calories 384 cal
Protein 18 g
Fibre 16 g
Fat 23 g
Saturated Fat 6 g
Carbs 32 g
Sugar 17 g

GF | V | EF

Mediterranean eggplants with pumpkin & spinach mash

Serves 2 | Preparation time: 10 minutes | Cooking time: 30 minutes

1 large eggplant (aubergine),
sliced in half

50 g (1¾ oz) feta, crumbled

40 g (1½ oz/¼ cup) toasted
almonds, chopped

40 g (1½ oz/¼ cup) sun-dried
(sun-blushed) tomatoes,
chopped

1 lemon, cut into wedges

1 red onion, chopped

PUMPKIN & SPINACH MASH

400 g (14 oz) pumpkin (winter
squash), peeled and cut into 1
cm (½ in) cubes

15 g (½ oz) salted butter

125 ml (4 fl oz/½ cup) full-cream
(whole) milk

100 g (3½ oz/2 cups) English
spinach leaves

1 teaspoon sea salt

Eggplants are a great heart-healthy food, rich in fibre, which is essential for maintaining a healthy digestive system. You'll also love our take on pumpkin mash, with more hidden vegetables – our speciality.

Preheat the oven to 180°C (350°F) and line a baking tray with baking paper.

Lay the eggplant halves skin-side down on the prepared baking tray and roast for 20 minutes until soft. Remove from the oven and leave to cool slightly, then scrape out the flesh with a spoon into a bowl, reserving the hollowed-out skins.

Add the feta, almonds and sun-dried tomatoes to the bowl with the cooked eggplant and mix together well, then spoon the mixture back into the eggplant skins. Top each eggplant half with a lemon wedge and scatter over the red onion, then bake in the oven for 10 minutes until nicely golden.

Meanwhile, make the pumpkin and spinach mash. Bring a saucepan of water to a boil, add the pumpkin and boil for 10 minutes or until soft when pricked with a fork. Drain and return to the pan with the butter and milk and mash well until smooth. Stir in the spinach and salt.

Spoon the mash onto plates and serve alongside the eggplant halves together with extra lemon wedges for squeezing.

nutritional info:
Energy 1569 kj
Calories 375 cal
Protein 15 g
Fibre 9 g
Fat 24 g
Saturated Fat 8 g
Carbs 38 g
Sugar 18 g

GF | V | EF

Mexican beef tortillas

Serves 4 | Preparation time: 5 minutes | Cooking time: 8 hours

1 teaspoon paprika

1 teaspoon chilli powder

1 teaspoon onion powder

1 teaspoon garlic powder

1 x 750 g (1 lb 11 oz) chuck casserole steak

250 ml (8½ fl oz/1 cup) beef stock

1 tablespoon coconut aminos

150 g (5½ oz) cherry tomatoes, quartered

sea salt and freshly ground black pepper

½ red onion diced

½ red chilli, finely diced

½ bunch of coriander (cilantro) leaves, roughly chopped

50 g (1¾ oz) goat's feta

2 avocados, diced

juice of 1 lime

1 tablespoon olive oil

TO SERVE

1 large iceberg lettuce, leaves separated

GF | NF | EF

We love iceberg lettuce cups as a lower carbohydrate substitute for traditional tortillas. This recipe works just as well in the oven as the slow cooker so you can make the decision based on what's in your kitchen.

Combine the paprika and the chilli, onion and garlic powders in a large bowl, add the beef and rub all over.

Transfer the beef to a slow cooker, add the beef stock, coconut aminos and half the tomatoes, then season well and cook on low for 8 hours, or until the meat is tender and almost falling apart. Alternatively, add the ingredients to a roasting tin, cover with foil and cook in an oven preheated to 140°C (275°F) for 3½ hours. Keeping the beef in the slow cooker or roasting tin, take two forks and shred the meat roughly. Set aside.

Combine the remaining cherry tomatoes and the red onion, chilli, coriander, goat's feta and avocado together in a bowl to make a salsa. Dress with the lime juice and olive oil and season well with salt and pepper.

Arrange the shredded meat, salsa and lettuce leaves on the table in bowls. To serve, take a lettuce leaf and spoon over a few tablespoonfuls of the shredded beef, then top with a tablespoonful of salsa and finally fold the leaf up to finish the tortilla. Enjoy!

nutritional info:
Energy 1499 kj
Calories 359 cal
Protein 27 g
Fibre 2 g
Fat 25 g
Saturated Fat 10 g
Carbs 10 g
Sugar 5 g

Coconut fish & sweet potato chips with rocket & tomato salad

Serves 2 | Preparation time: 10 minutes | Cooking time: 20 minutes

1 egg, lightly beaten

3 tablespoons ground almonds

3 tablespoons desiccated (shredded) coconut

2 x 100 g (3½ oz) firm white fish fillets such as snapper or barramundi

SWEET POTATO CHIPS

100 g (3½ oz) sweet potato, peeled and cut lengthways into 1 cm (½ in) thick slices

1 teaspoon sea salt

1 teaspoon chopped rosemary

2 tablespoons coconut oil, melted

ROCKET & TOMATO SALAD

2 handfuls of rocket (arugula)

75 g (2¾ oz) cherry tomatoes

1 teaspoon olive oil

Who doesn't love fish and chips? I certainly do, and I don't want to have to pass up on indulging in this favourite of mine just because I'm eating healthily. The sweet potato chips here are not only delicious but are also a wonderful source of slow-release energy, helping to prevent the blood sugar spikes linked to weight gain that can often result from eating carbohydrate-rich foods.

Preheat the oven to 180°C (350°F). Line a baking tray with baking paper.

Add the beaten egg to a shallow bowl. Add the ground almonds and desiccated coconut to a second shallow bowl and mix together well.

Dip the fish fillets first in the egg mixture, then into the ground almonds and coconut mixture to coat evenly. Place the coated fillets on one of the prepared baking trays and bake for 10–15 minutes, turning halfway through cooking, until cooked through and nicely golden.

Meanwhile, add the sweet potato slices, salt, rosemary and coconut oil to another baking tray and mix together well to coat evenly. Cook for 20 minutes, or until golden brown.

Toss the salad ingredients together in a bowl and serve alongside the fish and chips.

nutritional info:
Energy 1666 kj
Calories 399 cal
Protein 9 g
Fibre 4 g
Fat 13 g
Saturated Fat 10 g
Carbs 22 g
Sugar 10 g

GF | DF

Marinated lamb skewers

Serves 2 | Preparation time: 4 minutes plus marinating | Cooking time: 6 minutes

220 g (8 oz) lamb loin fillet, cut into small cubes

1 red capsicum (bell pepper), seeds removed and cut into 2.5 cm (1 in) pieces

1 red onion, quartered

1 zucchini (courgette), cut into 2.5 cm (1 in) pieces

MARINADE

1 teaspoon dried oregano

60 ml (2 fl oz/¼ cup) olive oil

1 garlic clove, finely chopped

zest and juice of ½ lemon

SALAD

½ baby cos (romaine) lettuce head, leaves separated

100 g (3½ oz) cherry tomatoes, quartered

½ cucumber, diced

1½ teaspoons olive oil

juice of ½ lemon

sea salt and freshly ground black pepper

GF | DF | EF | NF

Full of bright, citrusy flavour, these juicy skewers prove that kebabs don't always have to be unhealthy to be delicious. The recipe makes more marinade than you need here – keep the extra and use it later for coating fish for baking or marinating chicken.

Soak 4 bamboo skewers in cold water for 30 minutes.

Combine the marinade ingredients in a bowl and mix well.

Add the lamb pieces to a large bowl, pour over a third of the marinade and turn until well coated. Cover and marinate in the refrigerator for 4–6 hours.

Heat a barbecue chargrill or chargrill pan to medium–high.

Alternately thread the capsicum, onion, zucchini and marinated lamb pieces onto the skewers. Chargrill for 6 minutes, turning each minute, until cooked through. Set aside.

For the salad, put all the ingredients in a large bowl and toss together well. Season to taste.

To serve, arrange the salad on a serving platter and top with the lamb skewers.

nutritional info:
Energy 1769 kj
Calories 423 cal
Protein 24 g
Fibre 5 g
Fat 29 g
Saturated Fat 5 g
Carbs 19 g
Sugar 9 g

Pan-fried chicken with roasted vegetable salad

Serves 2 | Preparation time: 10 minutes | Cooking time: 20 minutes

1 tablespoon olive oil

1 garlic clove, crushed

1 red onion, finely chopped

200 g (7 oz) boneless, skinless chicken thighs, chopped

sea salt and freshly ground black pepper

½ broccoli head, florets roughly chopped

2 teaspoons dijon mustard

1 tablespoon apple cider vinegar

2 tablespoons chopped coriander (cilantro) leaves

ROASTED VEGETABLE SALAD

100 g (3½ oz) sweet potato, chopped into small cubes

150 g (5½ oz) baby new potatoes, chopped into quarters

1 carrot, cut into rough chunks

1 tablespoon olive oil

sea salt and freshly ground black pepper

50 g (1¾ oz/1 cup) English spinach leaves

GF | NF | EF | DF

We've used chicken as the protein in this salad, but beef and lamb will also work really well. I haven't met a person who doesn't like white potato, so I'm confident this will become a weekly staple.

Preheat the oven to 180°C (350°F) and line a baking tray with baking paper.

To make the roasted vegetable salad, arrange the sweet potato, potato and carrot pieces on the prepared baking tray, drizzle over the olive oil and season with salt and pepper. Bake for 30 minutes until softened and golden.

Meanwhile, heat the olive oil in a frying pan over a medium heat. Add the garlic and onion and sauté for 3–4 minutes, or until softened. Add the chicken pieces, season and sauté for 3–4 minutes until browned on all sides.

Add the chopped broccoli to the pan together with 1–2 tablespoons water and cook for 5 minutes, or until the liquid has evaporated and the broccoli is tender. Remove from the heat and stir through the mustard, apple cider vinegar and coriander.

Toss the spinach through the roasted vegetables and divide between plates. Top with the chicken and broccoli mixture and serve immediately.

nutritional info:
Energy 1780 kj
Calories 432 cal
Protein 28 g
Fibre 5 g
Fat 15 g
Saturated Fat 2 g
Carbs 41 g
Sugar 5 g

Baked ocean trout on pea mash

Serves 2 | Preparation time: 5 minutes | Cooking time: 10 minutes

200 g (7 oz) frozen peas

15 g (½ oz) salted butter

juice and zest of 1 lemon

1 teaspoon chopped parsley, plus extra to serve

1 tablespoon coconut oil

2 x 125 g (4½ oz) ocean trout

sea salt and freshly ground black pepper

The health benefits of oily fish are huge. They contain extremely high amounts of the heart-healthy omega-3 fats that are key for improving your brain health, memory and cognition. Omega 3s are essential fatty acids, which means your body can't make them on its own, so you have to get them from food.

Add the peas to a saucepan of boiling water and cook for 2–3 minutes, until the peas are tender. Drain and return to the saucepan with the butter and stir to combine, then add the lemon juice, zest and half the parsley and mash together roughly with a fork. Set aside.

Melt the coconut oil in a frying pan over a medium–high heat. Add the ocean trout fillets skin-side down and cook for 2–4 minutes, until the skin is crispy. Turn with a spatula and cook for a further 2–3 minutes, until the ocean trout is cooked but still remains a little pink in the centre. Season.

Divide the mash between plates and top with the ocean trout, scattering over a little extra chopped parsley if you like.

nutritional info:
Energy 1619 kj
Calories 387 cal
Protein 28 g
Fibre 8 g
Fat 24 g
Saturated Fat 12 g
Carbs 21 g
Sugar 6 g

GF | EF | NF

Malaysian fish curry with cauliflower rice

Serves 4 | Preparation time: 10 minutes | Cooking time: 30 minutes

2 red chillies, deseeded and roughly chopped

2 garlic cloves, roughly chopped

1 lemongrass stem, white part only, roughly chopped

1 teaspoon curry powder

1 teaspoon ground turmeric

2 tablespoons coconut oil

1 x 400 ml (13½ fl oz) tin coconut milk

270 ml (9 fl oz) coconut cream

1 small sweet potato, diced

2 x 100 g (3½ oz) firm white fish fillets such as whiting, cut into 2 cm (¾ in) pieces

handful of green beans, chopped

1 small zucchini (courgette), chopped

coriander (cilantro) leaves, to garnish

CAULIFLOWER RICE

1 cauliflower head, cut into large florets

1 teaspoon coconut oil

GF | NF | EF | DF

This fish curry is full of warming spices and creamy, coconutty flavour. Feel free to substitute the fish for chicken breast pieces if you prefer – simply add them to the curry at the same time as the sweet potato and proceed as before. You can make the spice paste ahead of time if you want to be really efficient.

For the cauliflower rice, place the cauliflower florets in a food processor and blitz together briefly into rice-like pieces. Set aside.

Add the chilli, garlic and lemongrass to a food processor with the spices and 1 tablespoon coconut oil. Whiz together to form a paste.

Heat the remaining 1 tablespoon oil in a large saucepan over a medium heat, add the paste and cook for 2 minutes, or until fragrant. Add the coconut milk, coconut cream and sweet potato and simmer for 15 minutes, or until the sweet potato is soft. Add the fish pieces and simmer for a further 10–15 minutes until cooked, adding the beans and zucchini for the final 5 minutes of cooking .

Meanwhile, finish the cauliflower rice. Melt the coconut oil in a non-stick frying pan over a low–medium heat. Add the cauliflower, cover with a lid and cook for 5 minutes until soft.

Ladle the fish curry into bowls and garnish with a few coriander leaves. Serve with the cauliflower rice.

nutritional info:
Energy 2195 kj
Calories 524 cal
Protein 21 g
Fibre 8 g
Fat 42 g
Saturated Fat 37 g
Carbs 13 g
Sugar 10 g

Quinoa, sweet potato & beetroot salad with haloumi

Serves 1 | Preparation time: 15 minutes | Cooking time: 20 minutes

1 small sweet potato, cut into large chunks

1 small baby beetroot, cut into large chunks

1½ teaspoons coconut oil, melted

sea salt and freshly ground black pepper

3 tablespoons quinoa

handful of baby spinach leaves, torn

1½ teaspoons chopped flat-leaf (Italian) parsley

1½ teaspoons pepitas (pumpkin seeds)

30 g (1 oz) haloumi, cut into 1 cm (½ in) thick slices

juice of ½ lemon

Haloumi is one of my favourite cheeses – made from a combination of sheep's and goat's milk, it is easier on the digestive system than cow's milk cheeses, making it good for those with mild dairy sensitivity or intolerance.

Preheat the oven to 200°C (400°F).

Arrange the sweet potato and beetroot pieces on a baking tray, drizzle over the melted coconut oil and toss to combine. Season generously and roast for 20 minutes, or until tender. Remove from the oven and transfer to a large bowl.

Meanwhile, bring 250 ml (8½ fl oz/1 cup) water to the boil in a saucepan, add the quinoa, cover with a lid and cook for 15 minutes, fluffing up the grains halfway through cooking with a fork for extra volume, until the grains are tender and the water has been absorbed. Set aside to cool.

Once cool, add the cooked quinoa, spinach, parsley and pepitas to the bowl with the sweet potato and beetroot pieces and toss well to combine.

Heat a non-stick frying pan over a high heat, add the haloumi slices and dry-fry for 2–3 minutes on each side until golden. Remove from the pan and use to top the salad, squeezing over the lemon juice to finish. Enjoy.

nutritional info:
**Energy 1715 kj
Calories 410 cal
Protein 18 g
Fibre 6 g
Fat 20 g
Saturated Fat 7 g
Carbs 45 g
Sugar 5 g**

GF | V | EF | NF

Slow-cooked lamb with sautéed greens

Serves 6 | Preparation time: 5 minutes | Cooking time: 3½–8 hours

3 garlic cloves, peeled

2 tablespoons chopped rosemary

1 x 1.5 kg (3 lb 5 oz) lamb shoulder

sea salt and freshly ground black pepper

1 tablespoon coconut oil

2 zucchini (courgettes), diced

200 g (7 oz) broccolini, sliced in quarters

100 g (3½ oz) Tuscan kale (cavolo nero), diced

This lamb is so tender and flavoursome that you don't need to load up on potatoes. By all means you can add them as a side but keep the focus of your plate on vegetables and quality protein.

Arrange the garlic cloves and rosemary over the base of a large slow cooker, lay over the lamb shoulder and season generously. Cook on low for 8 hours, or until the meat falls apart when pressed with a fork. Alternatively, add the ingredients to a casserole dish or a roasting tin, cover with a lid or foil and cook in an oven preheated to 140°C (275°F) for 3½ hours.

Melt the coconut oil in a large frying pan over a medium heat. Add the greens and sauté for 3 minutes, until tender. Remove from the heat and pile onto serving plates.

Gently shred the lamb with two forks and divide the meat among the plates. Serve.

GF | DF | EF | NF

nutritional info:
Energy 1950 kj
Calories 466 cal
Protein 51 g
Fibre 1 g
Fat 27 g
Saturated Fat 12 g
Carbs 9 g
Sugar 2 g

Baked fish with rocket, tomato & tahini

Serves 2 | Preparation time: 10 minutes | Cooking time: 10 minutes

2 x 100 g (3½ oz) firm white fish fillets such as snapper or barramundi, skin on

1 teaspoon olive oil

sea salt and freshly ground black pepper

2 handfuls of rocket (arugula)

6 cherry tomatoes, quartered

2 tablespoons chopped flat-leaf (Italian) parsley

2 tablespoons chopped basil

30 g (1 oz/⅓ cup) flaked almonds

½ avocado, diced

TAHINI DRESSING

2 tablespoons tahini

2 teaspoons olive oil

2 tablespoons apple cider vinegar

juice of ½ lemon

sea salt and freshly ground black pepper

Tahini is a paste made from sesame seeds and is one of the highest plant-based sources of calcium there is. I like to use tahini that is made from unhulled sesame seeds as it's more nutrient-rich than the hulled kind – try to seek it out if you can.

Preheat the oven to 200°C (400°F).

Take two pieces of foil large enough to wrap each piece of fish and place a square of baking paper in the centre of each. Place the fish fillets skin-side down on the baking paper, drizzle over the oil and season well, then wrap up the foil and seal tightly to form individual parcels.

Transfer the fish parcels to a large baking tray and bake for 10 minutes. Check to see if the fish is cooked to your liking by taking one of the parcels out of the oven and opening it up to check – if it needs longer, simply seal the foil back up and return to the oven for a few extra minutes.

Meanwhile make the tahini dressing by adding all the ingredients to a bowl with 1 tablespoon water and whisking together until smooth and creamy. (If you like a thinner dressing consistency, whisk in a little extra water.)

Add the rocket, cherry tomatoes, parsley, basil, flaked almonds and avocado to a bowl and toss gently to combine. Divide the salad between plates, top with the fish fillets and drizzle over the tahini dressing to serve.

nutritional info:
Energy 1850 kj
Calories 442 cal
Protein 30 g
Fibre 5 g
Fat 27 g
Saturated Fat 4 g
Carbs 11 g
Sugar 5 g

GF | DF | EF

Chickpea & pumpkin pilaf

Serves 2 | Preparation time: 10 minutes | Cooking time: 30 minutes

2 tablespoons olive oil

3 garlic cloves, crushed

1 small red onion, finely chopped

2 tablespoons tomato paste (concentrated purée)

1 tablespoon ground coriander

1 teaspoon ground cumin

1 teaspoon sea salt

155 g (5½ oz/1 cup) pumpkin (winter squash), finely diced

200 g (7 oz) tinned chickpeas, rinsed and drained

500 ml (17 fl oz/2 cups) vegetable stock

100 g (3½ oz/2 cups) English spinach leaves

125 ml (4 fl oz/½ cup) coconut milk

Chickpeas are a versatile vegetarian protein, rich in fibre and antioxidants. This is another of my favourite Meat Free Monday meals.

Add the olive oil, garlic and onion to a saucepan over a high heat and sauté for 2–3 minutes until softened. Stir in the tomato paste, coriander, cumin and salt and cook, stirring for 3 minutes, until the spices are fragrant, then add the pumpkin and sauté for a further 2 minutes.

Stir in the chickpeas and pour over the vegetable stock, then cover and bring to the boil. Reduce the heat to a simmer and cook for 20 minutes, or until the pumpkin is cooked through.

To finish, stir in the spinach leaves and coconut milk and mix together well. Spoon into bowls and serve.

nutritional info:
Energy 1669 kj
Calories 399 cal
Protein 11 g
Fibre 8 g
Fat 25 g
Saturated Fat 12 g
Carbs 36 g
Sugar 9 g

GF | V | VE | DF | EF | NF

Steak with pear, broccoli & rocket

Serves 1 | Preparation time: 5 minutes plus marinating | Cooking time: 8 minutes

½ broccoli head, florets chopped

1 x 100 g (3½ oz) scotch fillet steak

1 teaspoon olive oil

pinch of sea salt

pinch of freshly ground black pepper

2 handfuls of rocket (arugula)

1 tablespoon chopped walnuts

15 g (½ oz) goat's feta, crumbled

½ pear, finely sliced

You may have grown up disliking broccoli like me, but it's worth learning to love for its nutrient density and simplicity. Try this recipe and I'm confident you will be pleasantly surprised.

Add the broccoli to a steamer set over simmering water and steam for 5–6 minutes, or until just tender. Set aside.

Put the steak in a bowl, pour over the olive oil and add the salt and pepper. Cover with plastic wrap and leave to marinate for 1–2 hours.

Once marinated, drain the marinade into a chargrill pan set over a medium–high heat. Add the steak and cook to your liking – 2–4 minutes per side, depending on your desired result.

Place the rocket, walnuts, feta, pear and broccoli in a bowl and toss to combine.

Pile the salad onto a plate and serve with the steak.

nutritional info:
Energy 1618 kj
Calories 385 cal
Protein 30 g
Fibre 7 g
Fat 21 g
Saturated Fat 7 g
Carbs 22 g
Sugar 11 g

GF | EF

Lamb cutlets with warm broccoli salad

Serves 4 | Preparation time: 5 minutes | Cooking time: 10 minutes

2 broccoli heads, broken into florets

2 handfuls of rocket (arugula)

1 avocado, diced

30 g (1 oz/¼ cup) pepitas (pumpkin seeds)

2 tablespoons olive oil

juice of ½ lemon

30 g (1 oz) goat's feta, crumbled (optional)

8 x 50 g (1¾ oz) lamb cutlets

sea salt and freshly ground black pepper

Our warm broccoli salad is one you will use for years to come. The combination of broccoli and rocket provides powerful antioxidants, benefiting cell and skin health.

Bring a large saucepan of water to the boil, add the broccoli and blanch for 3–4 minutes, or until just tender. Drain, then transfer to a large bowl with the rocket, avocado and pepitas and toss together to combine.

In a small bowl, whisk the olive oil and lemon juice together in a bowl to make a dressing. Pour the dressing over the salad and scatter over the feta, if using. Toss to combine.

Heat a barbecue grill or chargrill pan to high. Season the lamb cutlets all over with salt and pepper, then transfer to the hot grill and cook for 3 minutes on each side until golden. Remove from the heat and serve with the warm broccoli salad.

nutritional info:
Energy 1883 kj
Calories 450 cal
Protein 40 g
Fibre 6 g
Fat 32 g
Saturated Fat 10 g
Carbs 10 g
Sugar 1 g

GF | EF | NF

Sausages with brussels slaw

Serves 4 | Preparation time: 5 minutes | Cooking time: 20 minutes

8 good-quality beef sausages

BRUSSELS SLAW

¼ red cabbage, shredded

2 carrots, grated

1 beetroot, grated

50 g (1¾ oz) baby spinach leaves, roughly chopped

1 tablespoon chopped parsley

20 g (¾ oz) salted butter

8 brussels sprouts, sliced

3 tablespoons Clean Mayonnaise (see below)

sea salt and freshly ground black pepper

CLEAN MAYONNAISE

1 large egg

juice of ½ lemon

1 tablespoon apple cider vinegar

1 teaspoon dijon mustard

¼ teaspoon sea salt

185 ml (6 fl oz/¾ cup) macadamia oil or olive oil

GF

Sausages were once considered unhealthy as they were traditionally made with fatty leftover animal parts and wrapped in intestines. In more recent times we have access to quality sausages made from grass-fed meats, that are free from preservatives and wrapped in a natural casing. To source quality snags, speak to your local butcher or look for labels containing the terms free range and grass fed at the supermarket.

To make the mayo, add the egg, lemon juice, vinegar, mustard and salt to a tall glass jar. Slowly pour over the macadamia oil, blending with a hand-held blender, until all the oil has been incorporated and the mayo is thick and runny.

For the brussel slaw, combine the cabbage, carrot, beetroot, spinach and parsley in a large bowl. Melt the butter in a large frying pan over a medium heat, add the sliced sprouts and sauté for 4–5 minutes until tender, then transfer to the bowl with the veg. Add the mayonnaise and toss together well to ensure everything is evenly coated. Season to taste.

Heat a barbecue chargrill or chargrill pan to medium–high. Add the sausages to the grill and cook for 15 minutes, turning every couple of minutes, until golden and cooked through. Serve immediately with the brussel slaw.

nutritional info:
Energy 1573 kj
Calories 376 cal
Protein 31 g
Fibre 7 g
Fat 27 g
Saturated Fat 9 g
Carbs 19 g
Sugar 8 g

Oven baked steak with sweet potato, tomato & spinach

Serves 2 | Preparation time: 5 minutes | Cooking time: 30 minutes

1 x 300 g (10½ oz) eye fillet steak

sea salt and freshly ground black pepper

1 tablespoon pine nuts

2 teaspoons coconut oil

150 g (5½ oz) sweet potato, cut into thin wedges

1 sprig rosemary

250 g (9 oz) cherry tomatoes

50 g (1¾ oz/1 cup) English spinach leaves

2 teaspoons dijon mustard

Preheat the oven to 200°C (400°F).

Remove the steak from the fridge and cut it in half, then season with salt and pepper on both sides and set aside to come to room temperature.

Heat a frying pan over a medium heat, add the pine nuts and toast for 2–3 minutes until lightly golden. Remove from the pan and set aside.

Heat ½ teaspoon of the coconut oil in a flameproof baking dish over a very high heat until smoking. Add the steaks and sear for 2 minutes on either side to brown, then remove from the dish and set aside.

Add the sweet potato pieces to the baking dish together with the rosemary and remaining oil and toss to combine. Bake for 20 minutes, turning once or twice as you go, until the potato starts to soften. Add the steak and tomatoes to the centre of the baking dish, pushing the sweet potato pieces to the side, and cook for a further 10 minutes, or until the sweet potato pieces are lightly golden, the tomatoes are soft and the steak is nicely medium-rare.

Remove the steak from the dish and transfer to a chopping board to rest for 2–3 minutes. Turn off the oven and place the baking dish with the chips and tomatoes in it to keep warm.

Once rested, cut the steak into thin slices and arrange on individual serving plates. Add the spinach and the toasted pine nuts to the baking dish, toss everything together well and season to taste, then divide the vegetable mixture between the plates. Serve with the dijon mustard.

nutritional info:
Energy 1632 kj
Calories 388 cal
Protein 40 g
Fibre 5 g
Fat 46 g
Saturated Fat 19 g
Carbs 25 g
Sugar 9 g

GF | DF | EF

Baked salmon with zucchini, kale & avocado cashew cream

Serves 2 | Preparation time: 10 minutes | Cooking time: 20 minutes

2 x 125 g (4½ oz) salmon fillets, skin on

sea salt and freshly ground black pepper

2 zucchini (courgettes)

1 teaspoon coconut oil

½ bunch Tuscan kale (cavolo nero), roughly chopped

2 tablespoons beef stock or broth

AVOCADO CASHEW CREAM

80 g (2¾ oz/½ cup) cashews, soaked for 10 minutes in boiling water, drained and rinsed

½ avocado

2 tablespoons coconut oil

juice and zest of 1 lemon

½ fresh chilli, finely chopped

handful of basil leaves

sea salt and freshly ground black pepper

Avocado cashew cream is a delicious and versatile sauce that can also be used as a dip, a salad dressing, or a substitute to store-bought guacamole or sour cream. Cut up some veggie sticks to snack on with the avocado cashew cream so any leftovers don't go to waste.

Preheat the oven to 180°C (350°F) and line a baking tray with baking paper.

Place the salmon fillets on the prepared baking tray and season with salt and pepper. Bake for 15–20 minutes, or until just cooked through but still a little pink in the centre.

Meanwhile, make the avocado cashew cream. Add all the ingredients to a blender together with 2 tablespoons water and whiz together until smooth. Set aside.

Using a spiraliser, cut the zucchini into fine vegetable noodles. (If you do not own a spiraliser, simply shave the zucchini into thin slices with a vegetable peeler or a mandoline.)

Melt the coconut oil in a large frying pan over a medium heat. Add the zucchini noodles and sauté for 1–2 minutes until just softened, then stir in the kale, pour over the stock and toss together briefly until the kale is wilted.

To serve, divide the zucchini and kale mixture between plates and top with the salmon fillets and dollops of the avocado cashew cream. Serve.

nutritional info:
Energy 1912 kj
Calories 457 cal
Protein 30 g
Fibre 8 g
Fat 30 g
Saturated Fat 8 g
Carbs 23 g
Sugar 5 g

GF | DF | EF

Snacks.

There's no need to feel hungry when you've got these healthy snacks ready to go. Some are great to have before training, others after. And there are a few for special occasions here too.

Avocado & spinach dip

Serves 6 | Preparation time: 5 minutes

200 g (7 oz/4 cups) English spinach leaves

2 avocados, mashed

3 tablespoons olive oil

1 teaspoon sea salt

juice of 1 lemon

2 garlic cloves, crushed

½ green chilli, deseeded and chopped

handful of basil leaves

1 teaspoon paprika, plus extra to serve

veggie sticks and slices, to serve

Such a simple recipe – all you need to do is prepare the vegetables and combine all ingredients in a blender. This is a great substitute for store-bought dips that are often full of poor-quality ingredients and preservatives.

Place all the ingredients into a food processor and blend until well combined. If the mixture is a little too thick, add a tablespoon or so of water to thin it out to your liking.

Spoon the dip into a serving dish, sprinkle over a little extra paprika and enjoy with veggie sticks and slices.

A | GF | V | VE | NF | DF | EF

nutritional info:
Energy 602 kj
Calories 144 cal
Protein 2 g
Fibre 4 g
Fat 14 g
Saturated Fat 2 g
Carbs 5 g
Sugar 1 g

Pumpkin, spinach & pine nut egg cups

Makes 6 | Preparation time: 5 minutes | Cooking time: 35 minutes

60 g (2 oz) pumpkin (winter squash), cut into 2 cm (¾ in) cubes

1 teaspoon coconut oil, melted

sea salt and freshly ground black pepper

1 tablespoon pine nuts

6 eggs

2 handfuls of baby spinach leaves, finely chopped

handful of rocket (arugula)

30 g (1 oz) goat's feta, crumbled

These are one of my favourite variations on my original BYO Egg Cups (see page 173). The combo of pumpkin, spinach and pine nuts is a real winner, filling these portable snacks with loads of lovely nutrients and flavour.

Preheat the oven to 180°C (350°F) and grease a six-hole muffin tray with a little melted coconut oil.

Add the pumpkin and coconut oil to a baking tray, season with salt and pepper and mix together well. Roast in the oven for 20 minutes, or until soft and lightly golden. Set aside.

Heat a non-stick frying pan over a medium heat, add the pine nuts and toast for 2–3 minutes until lightly golden. Remove from the pan and set aside.

Beat the eggs together in a large bowl and season with salt and pepper.

Divide the pumpkin, spinach, pine nuts and rocket evenly between the muffin tin holes, then pour over the beaten egg mixture and sprinkle over the feta. Bake for 10–15 minutes, or until nicely puffed up and golden and cooked through.

Remove from the oven and leave to cool (the cups will sink a little at this point, but that's fine). Enjoy straightaway or keep in a suitable airtight container in the fridge for up to 5 days.

nutritional info:
Energy 460 kj
Calories 110 cal
Protein 8 g
Fibre 0 g
Fat 8 g
Saturated Fat 3 g
Carbs 2 g
Sugar 1 g

A | GF | V

Chocolate zucchini mini muffins

Makes 10 | Preparation time: 5 minutes | Cooking time: 10 minutes

2 tablespoons coconut flour

2 tablespoons cacao powder

1 teaspoon gluten-free baking powder

½ teaspoon baking soda

1 zucchini (courgette), grated

2 eggs

2 tablespoons rice malt syrup

½ teaspoon vanilla extract

2 tablespoons dark chocolate (80% cacao solids), chopped

1 tablespoon coconut oil, melted

Super versatile and seriously good for you, zucchini is one of my favourite vegetables. It works surprisingly well in sweet treats and snacks, and is a great way to sneak extra vitamins and minerals into muffins like this (just don't tell the kids).

Preheat the oven to 180°C (350°F). Lightly grease a 12-hole mini-muffin tray with a little melted coconut oil or line it with paper liners.

Put all the ingredients in a mixing bowl and stir together well to form a batter. Spoon the batter into the prepared muffin tray and bake for 10 minutes or until a skewer inserted into the centre of a muffin comes out clean. Remove from the oven, transfer to a wire rack and leave to cool before tucking in.

Keep in a suitable airtight container in the fridge for 5 days, or in the freezer for up to 2 months.

nutritional info:
Energy 294 kj
Calories 70 cal
Protein 2 g
Fibre 1 g
Fat 5 g
Saturated Fat 2 g
Carbs 4 g
Sugar 1 g

BT | GF | V | NF

Berry good snack

Serves 1 | Preparation time: 5 minutes

150 g (5½ oz) Greek-style yoghurt

150 g (5½ oz/1 cup) fresh strawberries, quartered

8 almonds, chopped

1 tablespoon chopped walnuts

1 teaspoon dried cranberries or apricots

I think this has to be my favourite snack recipe. It's extremely healthy but it feels more indulgent than vegetable sticks and dips. The sweetness from the berries is a great way to satisfy afternoon sweet cravings and, combined with almonds and walnuts, it will fill you up and stop you grazing throughout the afternoon.

Dollop the yoghurt into a bowl or serving glass and top with the strawberries, almonds, walnuts and cranberries. Simple!

A | GF | V | EF

nutritional info:
Energy 1014 kj
Calories 241 cal
Protein 18 g
Fibre 12 g
Fat 10 g
Saturated Fat 1 g
Carbs 15 g
Sugar 12 g

BYO egg cups

Makes 12 | **Preparation time: 10 minutes** | **Cooking time: 10 minutes**

12 large eggs

sea salt and freshly ground black pepper

1 portobello mushroom, finely chopped

10–12 sun-dried tomatoes, finely chopped

½ red capsicum (bell pepper), seeds removed and finely chopped

2 tablespoons finely chopped chives

200 g (7 oz) feta, cut into small cubes

Preheat the oven to 180°C (350°F) and lightly grease a 12-hole muffin tin with a little melted coconut oil.

Beat the eggs together in a large bowl and season with salt and pepper, then pour into the holes of the prepared muffin tin up to three-quarters full.

Divide the remaining ingredients evenly between the egg 'cups', then bake for 10 minutes, or until nicely puffed up, golden and cooked through. Remove from the oven and leave to cool (the cups will sink a little at this point, but that's fine). Enjoy straightaway or keep in a suitable airtight container in the fridge for up to 5 days.

nutritional info:
Energy 479 kj
Calories 114 cal
Protein 9 g
Fibre 1 g
Fat 8 g
Saturated Fat 3 g
Carbs 2 g
Sugar 2 g

A | V | GF | NF

Coconut chai latte

Serves 4 | Preparation time: 15 minutes | Cooking time: 5 minutes

1 cardamom pod, seeds extracted

8 cloves

4 black peppercorns

2 cinnamon sticks

1 tablespoon grated fresh ginger

500 ml (17 fl oz/2 cups) coconut milk

4 black tea bags

4 teaspoons rice malt syrup

Our chai latte is made from tea bags and spices so it is really simple and time-efficient, without the refined sugar that is often found in the powders many cafes use. We do count chai lattes as a snack – the reality is that they still contain energy, so they must be factored into your weight-loss goals.

Place the cardamom, cloves and peppercorns in a blender or spice grinder and whiz together briefly to form a powder.

Add the powdered spices to a saucepan with the cinnamon sticks, ginger, coconut milk and 500 ml (17 fl oz/2 cups) water. Bring to the boil, then remove from the heat and add the tea bags. Cover and leave to steep for 10 minutes.

Once steeped, pour the chai through a strainer into 4 cups, stirring a teaspoon of rice malt syrup into each before serving.

nutritional info:
Energy 665 kj
Calories 159 cal
Protein 2 g
Fibre 4 g
Fat 9 g
Saturated Fat 7 g
Carbs 22g
Sugar 6 g

BT | GF | V | VE | DF | EF | NF

Hot chilli chocolate

Serves 1 | Preparation time: 1 minute | Cooking time: 5 minutes

200 ml (7 fl oz) coconut milk

1 teaspoon cacao powder

pinch of chilli powder (or to taste)

100 ml (3½ fl oz) boiling water

1 teaspoon rice malt syrup, to serve (optional)

This is a take on a very popular 28 recipe, our Sugar Free Hot Chocolate. The addition of chilli gives this drink a great kick but it also speeds up your metabolism and assists your natural ability to burn fat.

Warm the coconut milk in a small saucepan over a low heat.

Add the cacao, chilli and boiling water to a large mug and stir together well, then pour over the warmed coconut milk. Serve, stirring through the rice malt syrup if you like things a little sweeter.

nutritional info:
Energy 770 kj
Calories 184 cal
Protein 1 g
Fibre 2 g
Fat 13 g
Saturated Fat 11 g
Carbs 13 g
Sugar 6 g

BT | GF | V | VE | DF | EF | NF

No-bake energy bars

Makes 10 | Preparation time 10 minutes | Cooking time: 10 minutes

1 tablespoon coconut oil, melted

150 g (5½ oz/1 cup) quinoa flakes

20 g (¾ oz/½ cup) coconut flakes

80 g (2¾ oz/½ cup) chopped almonds

2 tablespoons pepitas (pumpkin seeds)

2 tablespoons sunflower kernels or seeds

2 tablespoons goji berries

125 ml (4 fl oz/½ cup) rice malt syrup

¼ teaspoon sea salt

1 teaspoon vanilla extract

These super-easy energy bars are one of my most popular recipes and it's easy to understand why – they're perfect for taking on that long bike ride when you need something nourishing to keep you going. For a nut-free version, replace the almonds with the same quantity of extra pepitas or sunflower kernels.

Preheat the grill (broiler) to high. Grease a baking tray with the coconut oil and line a loaf tin with baking paper.

Arrange the quinoa flakes, coconut flakes, almonds and seeds onto the prepared tray in an even layer, place under the hot grill and toast for 5 minutes until nicely golden, stirring halfway through cooking.

Tip the toasted mix into a large bowl and stir through the goji berries. Set aside.

Add the rice malt syrup, salt and vanilla to a saucepan over a medium–high heat. Cook, stirring constantly for 4–5 minutes, until the syrup is thick and golden and just at boiling point (be careful not to overcook here as it can burn easily).

Pour the hot syrup over the toasted mix and stir to combine thoroughly. Leave to cool slightly, then transfer the mixture to the prepared loaf tin and press it down firmly in an even layer. Transfer to the fridge and leave until set, about 20 minutes.

Once set, remove the mix from the tin and cut into 8–10 bars. Store in an airtight container or wrap individually in plastic wrap to take with you for when you're on the go.

nutritional info:
**Energy 982 kj
Calories 235 cal
Protein 7 g
Fibre 3 g
Fat 12 g
Saturated Fat 3 g
Carbs 25 g
Sugar 3 g**

BT | GF | V | VE | DF | EF

Nutty bliss balls

Makes 12 | Preparation time: 5 minutes

55 g (2 oz/½ cup) ground almonds

45 g (1½ oz/½ cup) desiccated (shredded) coconut

80 g (2¾ oz/½ cup) sesame seeds, plus 2 tablespoons for coating

60 g (2 oz/½ cup) walnuts, finely chopped

4 tablespoons almond butter

3 tablespoons tahini

1 teaspoon vanilla extract

3 tablespoons honey

These are an absolute favourite of the 28ers as they only take 5 minutes to prepare and taste like dessert, without any refined sugar. They are best consumed before training due to the carb content.

Place all the ingredients apart from 2 tablespoons of the sesame seeds in a bowl and mix together well.

Place the remaining sesame seeds in a shallow bowl.

Roll tablespoonfuls of the mixture into balls, then roll the balls in the remaining sesame seeds to coat evenly. Store in the fridge in an airtight container for up to 3 weeks, or in the freezer for up to 2 months.

nutritional info:
Energy 429 kj
Calories 102 cal
Protein 6 g
Fibre 2 g
Fat 15 g
Saturated Fat 3 g
Carbs 9 g
Sugar 6 g

BT | GF | V | DF | EF

Cacao & bean muffins

Makes 9 | Preparation time: 5 minutes | Cooking time: 25 minutes

400 g (14 oz) tinned kidney beans, rinsed and drained

3 eggs

40 g (1½ oz/⅓ cup) cacao powder

1 teaspoon gluten-free baking powder

2 tablespoons honey

1 teaspoon vanilla extract

125 ml (4 fl oz/½ cup) almond milk or other nut milk of choice

3 tablespoons coconut oil, melted

55 g (2 oz/½ cup) ground almonds

65 g (2¼ oz/½ cup) buckwheat flour (or wholemeal flour if you can tolerate grains)

While it may seem a little strange to see kidney beans popping up in this muffin recipe I urge you to give it a go – as they get broken down in the food processor you'll never tell that they're in there, while the extra protein they bring to the table helps to curb the excessive spike in blood sugar that indulging in a treat like this might otherwise lead to.

Preheat the oven to 180°C (350°F) and line two 6-hole muffin tins with 9 paper liners.

Place all the ingredients except the ground almonds and buckwheat flour into a blender or food processor and whiz together to combine. Pour the mixture into a large bowl, add the ground almonds and buckwheat flour and stir to form a batter.

Spoon the batter into the lined muffin tins and bake for 25 minutes, or until a skewer inserted into the centre of a muffin comes out clean. Remove from the oven, transfer to a wire rack and leave to cool before tucking in.

Keep in a suitable airtight container in the fridge for 5 days, or in the freezer for up to 2 months.

nutritional info:
Energy 627 kj
Calories 149 cal
Protein 6 g
Fibre 3 g
Fat 8 g
Saturated Fat 4 g
Carbs 14 g
Sugar 4 g

BT | GF | V | DF

Mango chia pudding

Serves 4 | Preparation time: 20 minutes

1 mango, roughly chopped

125 ml (4 fl oz/½ cup) coconut milk

1 tablespoon rice malt syrup

juice of 1 lemon

40 g (1½ oz/⅓ cup) chia seeds

40 g (1½ oz/¼ cup) fresh blueberries, to serve

Chia pudding is a popular breakfast but it doubles as an excellent snack, especially before training. We make up a few serves at home so we are prepared for the week ahead.

Add the mango, coconut milk, rice malt syrup and lemon juice to a blender or food processor and whiz together for 1 minute or until well combined.

Pour the mango mixture into a suitable airtight container and stir in the chia seeds. Transfer to the refrigerator and leave to chill for 15 minutes, stirring occasionally.

Divide the chia pudding among bowls and top with the blueberries to serve. Any leftovers will keep stored in the refrigerator for up to 3 days.

nutritional info:
Energy 605 kj
Calories 144 cal
Protein 5 g
Fibre 8 g
Fat 5 g
Saturated Fat 2 g
Carbs 22 g
Sugar 14 g

BT | GF | V | VE | NF | DF | EF

Alex's vegan 'snickers' bites

Makes 12 | Preparation time: 50 minutes

BASE

50 g (1¾ oz/⅓ cup) macadamia nuts, plus 1 tablespoon crushed

100 g (3½ oz/⅔ cup) cashew nuts, plus 1 tablespoon crushed

5 large medjool dates, pitted

FILLING

90 g (3 oz/⅓ cup) almond butter

10 large medjool dates, pitted

2 teaspoons vanilla extract

1 tablespoon maple syrup

pinch of sea salt

TOPPING

125 ml (4 fl oz/½ cup) coconut oil, melted

40 g (1½ oz/⅓ cup) cacao powder

3 tablespoons maple syrup

1 teaspoon vanilla extract

T | V | VE | GF | EF | DF

My brother Alex is not vegan but he loves to create clean versions of traditional treats. His vegan snickers bites are so delicious, I think they're even better than the real thing. Be mindful to keep this to once or twice a week though. It's still a treat!

For the base, soak the whole macadamia and cashew nuts in a bowl of warm water for 30 minutes, then drain and add to a food processor with the dates. Blend together until everything is very well combined and the dates have broken down completely, then use to cover the base of 12 small or 6 large cupcake liners. Transfer to the freezer to chill and firm up.

To make the caramel, add the almond butter and dates to the food processor and pulse to combine, then add the vanilla, maple syrup and salt and pulse until smooth. Roll the mixture into balls using your hands and press into thin discs, then press into the cupcake liners over the base layer. Sprinkle over half the crushed macadamia and cashew nuts and press into the caramel, then return to the freezer to chill.

For the topping, add the melted coconut oil, cacao powder, maple syrup and vanilla extract to a bowl and mix together well to form a smooth, chocolatey syrup.

Remove the cupcake liners from the freezer and pour over the topping, then sprinkle over the remaining crushed nuts. Return to the freezer for 10–15 minutes or until set, then enjoy.
Store in the freezer in an airtight container for up to 2 weeks.

nutritional info:
Energy 886 kj
Calories 212 cal
Protein 4 g
Fibre 2 g
Fat 19 g
Saturated Fat 9 g
Carbs 7 g
Sugar 4 g

Anzac cookies

Makes 12 | Preparation time: 5 minutes | Cooking time: 15 minutes

100 g (3½ oz/1 cup) rolled (porridge) oats

75 g (2¾ oz/½ cup) wholemeal spelt flour

60 g (2 oz/⅔ cup) desiccated (shredded) coconut

55 g (2 oz) flaked almonds

½ teaspoon gluten-free baking powder

¼ teaspoon sea salt

½ teaspoon ground cinnamon

45 g (1½ oz) unsalted butter, melted

3 tablespoons honey

1 teaspoon vanilla extract

3 tablespoons warm water

These wheat-free, refined sugar-free takes on the nation's favourite biscuit make a fantastic snack. I love to have one before training to give myself the energy boost I need to get smashing those PBs.

Preheat the oven to 160°C (320°F) and line a baking tray with baking paper.

Add the dry ingredients to a large bowl and mix until well combined. Add the wet ingredients to a second bowl and mix together well. Make a well in the dry ingredient mixture, pour over the liquid mixture and stir to form a dough.

Roll a tablespoon of the dough into a ball, place it on the prepared baking tray and flatten it out with the palm of your hand into a circle. Repeat with the remaining dough, leaving 3 cm (1¼ in) between each cookie. Bake for 15 minutes until golden brown.

Remove from the oven and leave to cool and firm up on the baking tray before eating. Keep stored in an airtight container for up to 2 weeks.

nutritional info:
**Energy 611 kj
Calories 145 cal
Protein 3 g
Fibre 3 g
Fat 9 g
Saturated Fat 5 g
Carbs 14 g
Sugar 5 g**

BT | V | EF

Healthy raspberry crumble

Serves 6 | Preparation time: 5 minutes | Cooking time: 20 minutes

130 g (4½ oz/1 cup) coconut flour

55 g (2 oz/1 cup) coconut flakes

125 g (4½ oz/½ cup) unsalted butter, melted

125 ml (4 fl oz/½ cup) rice malt syrup

½ teaspoon sea salt

250 g (9 oz/2 cups) raspberries, fresh or frozen

My take on a traditional apple crumble uses raspberries and coconut flakes, making it lower in fructose than the original and fantastic when served with a scoop of coconut ice cream. The tartness of the berries here is offset perfectly by the addition of rice malt syrup.

Preheat the oven to 180°C (350°F).

Lightly grease a baking tray with a little coconut oil.

Add the coconut flour, coconut flakes, melted butter, rice malt syrup and salt to a bowl and mix together thoroughly to form a loose, crumbly mixture.

Arrange the raspberries on the prepared baking tray in an even layer. Scatter over the crumble topping, then press down firmly with your hands to compact it and push it into the fruit.

Bake for 20 minutes or until the crumble topping is golden brown. Remove from the oven and leave to cool slightly, then divide among bowls and serve.

nutritional info:
Energy 1607 kj
Calories 384 cal
Protein 4 g
Fibre 11 g
Fat 24 g
Saturated Fat 18 g
Carbs 38 g
Sugar 18 g

T | GF | V | EF | NF

Gluten-free zucchini & ginger bread

Makes 12 | Preparation time: 5 minutes | Cooking time: 25 minutes

200 g (7 oz/2 cups) ground almonds

1 teaspoon ground cinnamon

1 teaspoon gluten-free baking powder

½ teaspoon sea salt

1 tablespoon crystallised ginger, finely diced

1 large zucchini (courgette), unpeeled and grated

60 ml (2 fl oz/¼ cup) coconut oil, melted

60 ml (2 fl oz/¼ cup) rice malt syrup

2 eggs, beaten

unsalted butter, to serve

Rice malt syrup is a great natural sugar substitution as it is made from natural ingredients and is fructose free. This is important as fructose is the sugar that will make us store fat when consumed in excess. Rice malt syrup works as a 1:1 substitute to sugar, but as your taste buds change and your desire for sweet foods decrease (yes it will happen!) you will find yourself needing less and less.

Preheat the oven to 180°C (350°F). Lightly grease a 16 cm x 11 cm (6¼ in x 4¼ in) loaf (bar) tin with a little coconut oil.

Combine the ground almonds, cinnamon, baking powder, salt and ginger in a bowl. Add the zucchini, coconut oil and rice malt syrup and mix together well, then stir in the beaten eggs to form a batter.

Pour the batter into the prepared loaf tin and bake for 20–25 minutes or until golden on top and a skewer inserted into the centre of the loaf comes out clean. For best results, enjoy warm, fresh out of the oven, spread with butter. To store, cover in plastic wrap or keep in an airtight container for up to 7 days.

nutritional info:
Energy 820 kj
Calories 196 cal
Protein 6 g
Fibre 3 g
Fat 16 g
Saturated Fat 5 g
Carbs 10 g
Sugar 4 g

BT | GF | V | DF

Asparagus, pumpkin & feta frittata

Serves 6 | Preparation time: 5 minutes | Cooking time: 20 minutes

8 eggs

60 ml (2 fl oz/¼ cup) coconut cream

130 g (4½ oz) asparagus spears, trimmed and diced

60 g (2 oz) pumpkin (winter squash), grated

100 g (3½ oz) goat's feta, crumbled

½–1 tablespoon chilli flakes

¼ teaspoon sea salt

¼ teaspoon freshly ground black pepper

Frittatas are such a great snack as all you need to do is make one on a Sunday and you have snacks for the entire week. Asparagus is a spring vegetable that's delicious when in season.

Preheat the oven to 180°C (350°F). Grease a 20 cm (8 in) round cake tin with a little coconut oil.

Whisk the eggs and coconut cream together in a large bowl to combine, then whisk in the remaining ingredients.

Pour the frittata mixture into the prepared cake tin and cook for 20 minutes or until cooked through and firm to touch. Leave to cool slightly before slicing into wedges. Store in an airtight container in the fridge for 4–5 days.

nutritional info:
Energy 778 kj
Calories 186 cal
Protein 13 g
Fibre 1 g
Fat 13 g
Saturated Fat 31 g
Carbs 5 g
Sugar 2 g

A | GF | V | NF

Hidden veggie bread

Serves 12 | Preparation time: 5 minutes | Cooking time: 40 minutes

200 g (7 oz/2 cups) ground almonds

35 g (1¼ oz/¼ cup) buckwheat flour

2 tablespoons psyllium husks

1½ teaspoons gluten-free baking powder

¼ teaspoon sea salt

4 eggs, beaten

1 tablespoon apple cider vinegar

1 tablespoon rice malt syrup

60 ml (2 fl oz/¼ cup) coconut oil, melted

1 zucchini (courgette), grated

Our hidden veggie bread is another before-training winner. I like to make it on the weekend and portion slices out for the week. It also freezes well and is one the whole family will love.

Preheat the oven to 180°C (350°F). Lightly grease a 16 cm x 11 cm (6¼ in x 4¼ in) loaf (bar) tin with a little coconut oil.

Combine the ground almonds, buckwheat flour, psyllium husks, baking powder and salt in a large bowl.

In a second bowl, combine the eggs, vinegar, rice malt syrup and melted coconut oil.

Tip the wet ingredients into the dry mix and stir together well to form a batter. Leave to rest for 5 minutes, then stir in the zucchini and mix well.

Spoon the batter into the prepared loaf tin and bake for 35–40 minutes or until a skewer inserted into the centre of the loaf comes out clean. Enjoy warm fresh out of the oven or, for best results, toast under the grill (broiler). Store in an airtight container for up to 7 days, or slice and freeze in zip-lock bags for up to 3 months.

nutritional info:
Energy 833 kj
Calories 199 cal
Protein 7 g
Fibre 3 g
Fat 16 g
Saturated Fat 5 g
Carbs 7 g
Sugar 1 g

BT | GF | V | DF

Peanut butter sweet potato brownies

Makes 12 | **Preparation time: 30 minutes** | **Cooking time: 50 minutes**

1 sweet potato, cut into 1 cm (½ in) cubes

55 g (2 oz/½ cup) ground almonds

35 g (1¼ oz/¼ cup) buckwheat flour (or wholemeal flour if you can tolerate grains)

125 g (4½ oz/½ cup) peanut butter

40 g (1½ oz/⅓ cup) cacao powder

3 tablespoons coconut oil, melted

2 tablespoons honey

3 eggs

1 teaspoon vanilla extract

1 teaspoon gluten-free baking powder

As you know by now, I'm all for sneaking a little veggie into my sweet treats and these brownies are no exception. I like to use the leftover sweet potato here for adding to salads as an extra source of delicious slow-release energy.

Preheat the oven to 180°C (350°F). Grease a 20 cm x 20 cm (8 in x 8 in) baking tin with a little melted coconut oil.

Arrange the sweet potato pieces on a baking tray in an even layer. Roast for 20 minutes, or until soft when pricked with a fork.

Allow the sweet potato to cool for 10 minutes, then measure out 250 g (9 oz/1 cup).

Transfer the measured sweet potato to a large mixing bowl with all the remaining ingredients and mix together to form a batter. Pour the batter into the prepared tin and bake for 20 minutes, or until a cake skewer inserted into the centre of the tin comes out clean.

Remove from the oven and leave to cool in the tin before cutting into squares. The brownies will keep for up to 5 days in the fridge in an airtight container, or up to 2 months in the freezer.

nutritional info:
Energy 883 kj
Calories 211 cal
Protein 7 g
Fibre 3 g
Fat 14 g
Saturated Fat 5 g
Carbs 15 g
Sugar 6 g

T | GF | V | DF

Better than ice cream

Serves 3 | **Preparation time: 5 minutes**

2 bananas, cut into chunks and frozen

125 ml (4 fl oz/½ cup) coconut cream

2 tablespoons almonds

1 teaspoon ground cinnamon

1 tablespoon cacao powder

1 tablespoon rice malt syrup

This delicious natural alternative to store-bought ice cream is filled with good fats, complex carbohydrates and lovely magnesium-rich cacao. It's perfect for when you have one of those cravings for ice cream that just won't go away, and doesn't need any fancy equipment to make.

Place all of the ingredients in a high-speed blender together with 60 ml (2 fl oz/¼ cup) water and blend on high for at least 30 seconds, or until everything is well combined, smooth and creamy.

Divide the mixture among bowls and serve immediately. Alternatively, if you prefer a more solid ice cream-like texture, pour the mixture into a shallow dish and freeze for 1 hour before serving. Any leftovers can be kept stored in a suitable airtight container in the freezer for 2–3 days.

nutritional info:
Energy 999 kj
Calories 237 cal
Protein 3 g
Fibre 9 g
Fat 10 g
Saturated Fat 5 g
Carbs 38 g
Sugar 15 g

BT | GF | V | VE | DF | EF

Lemon & blueberry muffins

Makes 8 | Preparation time: 5 minutes | Cooking time: 30 minutes

6 eggs, beaten

1 teaspoon vanilla bean paste

3 tablespoons rice malt syrup

zest and juice of 1 lemon

60 ml (2 fl oz/¼ cup) coconut oil, melted

65 g (2¼ oz/½ cup) coconut flour

pinch of sea salt

2 teaspoons gluten-free baking powder

80 g (2¾ oz/½ cup) blueberries, fresh or frozen

These muffins are made using coconut flour and are the perfect nut-free snack and lunchbox treat. The combination of lemon and blueberry is one of my favourites!

Preheat the oven to 170°C (340°F) and line two 6-hole muffin tin with 8 paper liners.

Put the beaten eggs, vanilla bean paste, rice malt syrup, lemon juice and zest and coconut oil in a mixing bowl and mix well. Add the coconut flour, salt and baking powder and stir together well to form a batter, then gently fold in the blueberries.

Pour the mixture evenly into the paper liners and bake for 30 minutes, or until golden and a skewer inserted into the centre of a muffin comes out clean. Remove from the oven, transfer to a wire rack and leave to cool before tucking in.

Keep in a suitable airtight container in the fridge for 5 days, or in the freezer for up to 3 months.

nutritional info:
Energy 690 kj
Calories 165 cal
Protein 6 g
Fibre 3 g
Fat 12 g
Saturated Fat 8 g
Carbs 10 g
Sugar 4 g

BT | GF | V | DF | NF

Low-carb raspberry & coconut muffins

Makes 12 | Preparation time: 10 minutes | Cooking time: 30 minutes

255 g (9 oz/2½ cups) ground almonds

1 teaspoon ground cinnamon

1 teaspoon baking powder

4 eggs, beaten

60 ml (2 fl oz/¼ cup) coconut oil, melted

60 g (2 oz/¼ cup) granulated stevia blend or rice malt syrup

125 g (4½ oz/1 cup) fresh raspberries

15 g (½ oz/¼ cup) coconut flakes

Using ground almonds and stevia, these muffins are extremely low in carbohydrates and packed with protein and healthy fats. If you don't like the taste of stevia then use rice malt syrup or honey, but keep them to before training as this modification will increase the carbohydrate content.

Preheat the oven to 180°C (350°F). Lightly grease a 12-hole mini-muffin tray with a little melted coconut oil.

Combine the ground almonds, cinnamon and baking powder in a large bowl, then add the eggs, oil and stevia and mix together thoroughly to form a thickish batter. Carefully fold through the raspberries and coconut, adding a little water, if necessary, up to 250 ml (8½ fl oz/½ cup), to thin the batter if it is very thick.

Spoon the batter into the prepared muffin tray and bake for 30 minutes, or until a skewer inserted into the centre of a muffin comes out clean. Remove from the oven, transfer to a wire rack and leave to cool before tucking in.

Keep in a suitable airtight container in the fridge for 5 days, or in the freezer for up to 2 months.

nutritional info:
Energy 971 kj
Calories 232 cal
Protein 6 g
Fibre 5 g
Fat 20 g
Saturated Fat 8 g
Carbs 5 g
Sugar 2 g

A | BT | V | GF | DF

Nut-free bliss bites

Makes 8 | **Preparation time: 10 minutes**

250 g (9 oz) sunflower kernels

1 x 30 g (1 oz) scoop vanilla protein powder

1 teaspoon ground cinnamon

1 teaspoon vanilla extract

1 teaspoon natvia (stevia) powder

2 tablespoons tahini

2 tablespoons cacao powder

60 ml (2 fl oz/¼ cup) coconut oil, melted

1 tablespoon rice malt syrup

This nut-free snacking option tastes like dessert rolled into a ball. By using natvia – a plant extract you can find in the baking aisle of the supermarket – I've managed to keep the natural sugars low here, meaning that you can really get stuck into enjoying these blissful bites without the worry.

Place the sunflower kernels, protein powder, cinnamon, vanilla and natvia in a high-speed blender or food processor and whiz together to a rough powder. Transfer to a bowl, add the tahini, cacao, melted coconut oil and rice malt syrup and mix well.

Using an ice cream scoop or a spoon, shape the mixture into walnut-sized pieces, then roll each piece into a ball using your hands (to prevent sticking, lightly grease your hands with a little melted coconut oil first).

Arrange the balls on a plate and leave to chill and firm in the fridge for 20–30 minutes before serving. Store in the fridge in an airtight container for up to 2 weeks, or in the freezer for up to 3 months.

nutritional info:
Energy 715 kj
Calories 171 cal
Protein 6 g
Fibre 4 g
Fat 14 g
Saturated Fat 4 g
Carbs 7 g
Sugar 1 g

BT | GF | V | VE | DF | EF | NF

Raw cashew & chia protein bites

Makes 12 | Preparation time: 20 minutes

1 tablespoon chia seeds, plus extra for coating

250 g (9 oz) cashew nuts

1 x 30 g (1 oz) scoop chocolate whey protein powder, plus extra for coating

2 tablespoons cacao powder

1 tablespoon granulated stevia blend

1 teaspoon ground cinnamon

60 ml (2 fl oz/¼ cup) coconut oil, melted

These protein bites are high in both protein and energy, making them the perfect post-workout snack. You may find your willpower tested given how great they taste, but do try to stick to just one.

Add the chia seeds to a bowl, pour over 60 ml (2 fl oz/¼ cup) water and leave to soak for 10 minutes.

Meanwhile, add the cashew nuts, protein powder, cacao, stevia and cinnamon to a high-speed blender or food processor and pulse briefly to combine.

Tip the nut mixture into a large bowl, add the melted coconut oil and stir together to combine, then stir in the chia seed mixture.

Using your hands, form tablespoonfuls of the mixture into balls (adding a touch of melted coconut oil to your hands before doing so to prevent the mixture sticking). Sprinkle a few extra chia seeds or a little extra protein powder over the balls, then transfer to an airtight container and leave to chill in the fridge before serving. The balls will keep in the fridge for up to 7 days.

nutritional info:
Energy 780 kj
Calories 186 cal
Protein 6 g
Fibre 3 g
Fat 15 g
Saturated Fat 6 g
Carbs 6 g
Sugar 1 g

AT | V | GF | EF

Raw chocolate brownie bites

Makes 12 | **Preparation time: 10 minutes**

75 g (2¾ oz/¾ cup) walnut halves

40 g (1½ oz/¼ cup) almonds

8 pitted medjool dates

2 tablespoons cacao powder

2 tablespoons cacao nibs

2 tablespoons coconut flakes

1 teaspoon vanilla extract

Packed with cacao, high in magnesium and perfect for any sweet craving, these indulgent chocolate brownie bites are a favourite of Steph, our awesome nutritionist.

Place the walnuts and almonds in a high-speed blender or food processor and whiz to a fine flour-like consistency. Add the remaining ingredients and pulse together until crumbly and roughly textured. Transfer the mixture to a bowl.

With lightly greased hands, take a small handful of the mixture and roll into a ball. Transfer to a plate and repeat with the remaining mixture, then transfer the brownie bites to the refrigerator to chill and firm up for 20–30 minutes before serving. Store in the fridge in an airtight container for up to 2 weeks, or in the freezer for up to 3 months.

nutritional info:
Energy 623 kj
Calories 149 cal
Protein 3 g
Fibre 2 g
Fat 9 g
Saturated Fat 1 g
Carbs 18 g
Sugar 14 g

BT | GF | V | VE | DF | EF

Exercises.

28 minutes a day.

The 5 fitness levels:

1 **Rookie (20 secs working / 40 secs rest)**
With plenty of rest time, this one's great for total beginners to start working out, and to focus on learning and perfecting form and movements.

2 **Player (30 secs working / 30 secs rest)**
Been away from the gym for a bit? Ease yourself back into it with a 50/50 work/rest split, and polish your form while you're at it.

3 **Hotshot (40 secs working / 20 secs rest)**
Feeling pretty fit? Know your push-ups from your planks? Up for a bit of a challenge? Step up, Hotshot, this one's for you.

4 **Champ (50 secs working / 10 secs rest)**
My personal favourite! With only moments to catch your breath, you better know what you're about before you take this on.

5 **Maniac (Constant Burn)**
What, 28 minutes, no rest?! Surely not … Are you crazy? Why did I even make this level?

How to choose your fitness level

My levels are tailored to suit your fitness ability. Choose one that best resembles you, but remember you can level up or down.

You'll notice that the lower levels have more rest time between workouts. The reason for this is because while it's great to get out of your comfort zone, that comfort zone is still relative to your fitness level! So I've designed different recovery periods and a range of exercises within each level.

Why 28 minutes each day is enough

I have been training clients for this period of time and in this style for nearly 15 years and the results have been incredible. These are functional full-body workouts to push yourself. You WILL be able to find 28 minutes a day and get these sessions done. You have to shock your body to create change and break through plateaus.

1

Rookie
(as many quality reps as you can in 20 seconds)

1. **Chair squat**
   Stand straight, then with every rep, sit down on a bench or chair, focus on heels staying in contact with the floor.

2

2. **Stool or chair pushup**
   Keeping your body straight from head to toes (or to knees), breathe in as you lower your body and out as you push yourself up.

3. **Dumbbell curl and press**
   With a hammer grip, curl dumbbells to your shoulders, then press to a full extension above your head.

3

4. **Plank on knees**
Keep your butt squeezed, your tummy tight and head up and make sure you continue to breathe normally while you hold the position.

5. Alternating leg lowers
Exhale as you lower to each side. Always control the movement and keep your lower back in contact with the floor or mat.

6. Windmills
Be loose. Let your arms fly, hips and back rotate and open up through the chest more and more as you go.

7. Dancing feet
Keep your butt high and you should feel it through your achillies, calves and up the back of your legs.

Give me a break;
I'm so tired/grumpy/over it

Especially when they're starting out, people constantly use these excuses to cancel their exercise date with themselves. In reality, each and every one is the exact reason they should make some time to work out. Putting on your gear and starting is the hard part. Once you do, it's easy to keep going. Work hard and you'll focus completely on exercise and push all those frustrations to the back of your mind. When you're not feeling great emotionally – being sick is a whole other matter – exercise is the best thing you can do for yourself and I guarantee the world will feel like a better place when you're done.

Player

(as many quality reps as you can in 30 seconds)

1. **Static wall squat**
   Squat against the wall with hips and knees at 90 degrees, arms across your chest and head against the wall. Stay still with slow even breathing.

2. **Kneeling pushups**
   Ensure your hips and chest lower as one, breathe in as you go down and out as you come up.

3. **Dumbbell clean and press**
   Change hands every 5 reps.

4. Plank

Hold yourself flat on your forearms and toes. Keep your body straight from head to heels, squeeze your butt and make sure you don't hold your breath.

5. Alternating leg lowers

Focus on moving only one leg at a time and breathe out as you lower each leg.

6. Dumbbell boxing uppercuts
Continuous circular uppercuts right and left in a circular rhythmic motion.

7. Leg swings
Change legs every 5 reps. Swing your leg like a pendulum with a slight knee bend through the back swing to get a quad and hamstring stretch in one movement.

Hotshot

(as many quality reps as you can in 40 seconds)

1. Squats

Keep your knees out, push your butt back and make sure your heels do not lift off the ground.

1

2

2. Pushups

Work within a range you can handle, as many as you can on your toes but remember you can drop to your knees if you need to. Breathe in on the way down and out as you push yourself up.

3

4

5

3. Squat and press
Keep the dumbbells on your shoulders as you lower down and drive them up as you stand. Go slowly and keep your heels flat and back straight.

4. Plank up/downs
Make sure you are in a position with stability before moving. Perform this exercise slowly. Keep your head up and tummy tight at all times.

5. Scissor kicks
Position your legs at a realistic height. Lower is harder, so ensure you can perform the movement at that height without any arching in the lower back.

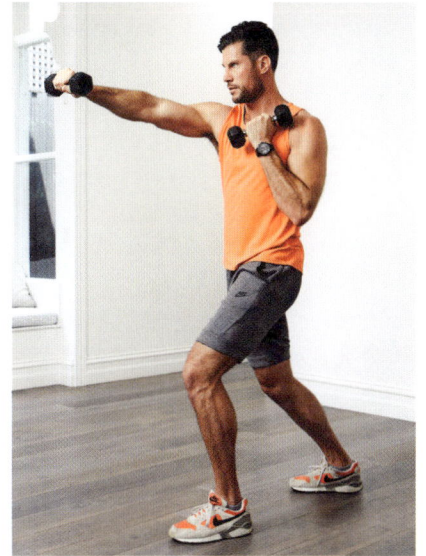

6

7

6. Boxing jabs
  Position your left foot forward
  if you are right handed and
  vice versa. Slightly bend your
  knee and rotate through the
  hips keeping the dumbbells in
  front of your face.

7. Inside outside swings
  With a relaxed upper body,
  let the leg swing like a
  pendulum. Swing higher as
  you loosen up. Repeat with
  the other leg.

1

Champp
(as many quality reps as you can in 50 seconds)

1. **Jump squats**
   Focus on a soft landing, absorbing the force, and springing into the next squat. Breathe out on every jump.

2. **Pushup knee touches**
   Complete a full pushup, then bring your left knee up to your left elbow, next bring your right knee up to your right elbow. Repeat. Quality slow movements are key.

2

3. Alternating lunge with curls

As you come up you curl up and as you go down you straighten your arms. Get your curl and lunges in sync. Always curl arms together but alternate legs.

4. Side planks

Aim to create a straight line from ankles, knees, hips and shoulders with your head back. Keep your hips up, butt squeezed and keep breathing. Repeat on both sides.

5. Leg lowers

Start with legs up as straight as you can, then lower slowly until nearly touching the floor. Pause and raise your legs again. This is a slow controlled movement, breathing out as you lower your legs. A slight knee bend and partial range is fine, just ensure you don't arch your back off the ground.

6

7

6. Kneeling overhead boxing
Be tall through your hips and torso and find a good boxing rhythm.

7. High knee jog
Work the arms hard, be light on your feet and get your knees as high as you can with every stride.

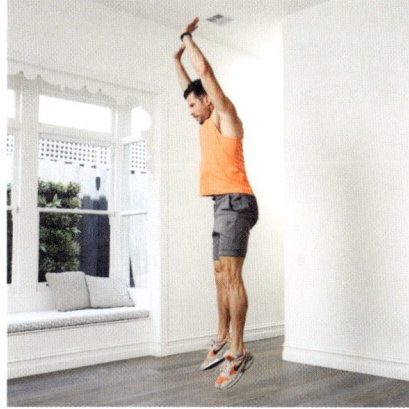

1

Maniac
(as many quality reps as you can in 60 seconds)

1. Burpees
Be light on your feet and slow the movement down as you need to, making sure you don't arch your back.

2. Clap/power pushups
Slowly lower yourself to a pushup position. Breathe out and explode up into a clap, then catch yourself with a soft landing, absorbing the impact, before exploding into the next rep. As you become fatigued, kneeling clap pushups are fine.

2